HISTORY

D-DAY
MINUTE BY MINUTE

Landing craft with their accompanying barrage balloons made their way toward Utah and Omaha Beaches for the invasion that came to be known as D-Day.

Commander Dwight D. Eisenhower visited with paratroopers to give them their orders before they set out to the beaches of Normandy for the D-Day invasion.

CONTENTS

An improvised monument to an American soldier who was killed during the June 6, 1944, invasion. A bronze statue created from this image now stands at the National D-Day Memorial in Bedford, Virginia.

Soldiers worked to operate a Signal Corps radio on an invasion beach. One cranked the generator, while another very young-looking serviceman spoke into the hand-held.

When Hitler started his campaign against Europe, his Wehrmacht was state-of-the-art, massive, and well equipped. A few years later, however, he was struggling to find men and resources to keep up the fight.

THE TURNING TIDE

After years of the Axis spreading war around the globe, the Allies were finally able to push back.

On September 1, 1939, Adolf Hitler's Wehrmacht invaded Poland, beginning World War II. France and Great Britain declared war on Germany, but the German-Soviet Nonaggression Pact (signed a week later) meant Hitler wouldn't face a second front in the east—yet. In accordance with the pact, the Soviets invaded from the east, and Poland fell. The Soviets and the Germans divided it up between them. The Wehrmacht swept through Europe, blitzing Norway, Denmark, Belgium, and the Netherlands in the north and moving into France in the south. Earlier in 1939, Benito Mussolini had signed the Pact of Steel with Hitler, making Italy part of the Axis powers. Hungary, Romania, and then Bulgaria joined the Axis, and Yugoslavia and Greece fell. If Hitler hadn't been so hungry to conquer more countries, he might have held on to his blood prizes.

But the madness that drove Hitler to try to exterminate the Jewish people and establish a "New Order" in Europe drove him to break his nonaggression pact with the Soviets. On June 22, 1941, he invaded the Soviet Union, forcing the Soviets to side with the Allies. On December 7, Germany's ally Japan bombed Pearl Harbor. The next day, America declared war on Japan, and soon the Axis declared war on America.

It was truly a world war, as the largely democratic Allies fought against the tyrannical Axis powers, with the Soviet Union as an uneasy but essential member of the Allies. In July 1942, Hitler ordered the capture of Stalingrad. When the battle for the city concluded in February 1943, the Soviets had inflicted enormous casualties on the Nazis (while suffering staggering losses themselves). By this time, the US was sending troops to the front lines. The tide had begun to turn. British and American forces pushed the Axis out of North Africa, then Sicily, then Italy, and Mussolini's government fell in July 1943.

While Germany once had supremacy in the air and ocean, it was losing its grasp on these battlegrounds. In 1942, the Allies targeted the Luftwaffe's fighting force and drove much of it back to Germany to defend the Fatherland from air raids. German U-boats (*Unterseeboote*, meaning "undersea boats") had once plagued the Allies in the Atlantic, but after Britain cracked Germany's Enigma code, the Allies decimated the Kriegsmarine and effectively regained control of the shipping lanes in the Atlantic. Supplies and troops began arriving en masse in England, allowing the Allies to stockpile, plan, and train for a full-scale invasion of occupied continental Europe.

WHAT A PLAN!

Operation Overlord involved multiple governments and millions of people, and the Allies had to keep all the details top secret during planning.

To win the war, the Allies needed to invade Western Europe. Everyone knew it. The Soviet Union knew it; Joseph Stalin had been demanding a second front in the west to take the pressure off his troops on the eastern front since the German invasion in 1941. America knew it; President Franklin D. Roosevelt had been promising the Soviets a western front since 1942. The British knew it; Prime Minister Winston Churchill was still doing his best, however, to put it off for as long as possible because his nation was war weary and couldn't afford any significant loss of manpower. The French knew it; they were willing to suffer more civilian casualties to get out from under Nazi occupation. And the Germans certainly knew it, as Adolf Hitler and General Erwin Rommel poured enormous amounts of resources into building their massive network of defenses known as the Atlantic Wall.

Everyone also knew an invasion was an all-or-nothing proposition. If the Allies failed to breach the Atlantic Wall and get a foothold in Europe, the war would drag on for at least another year—probably longer. Germany could not very likely win the war, but the one slim chance Hitler had was for the Soviets to feel betrayed if they didn't get a second front. The Germans had no hope of beating the Red Army, but if they could inflict enough casualties on

This map of Omaha Beach was created by the US Navy to show tide lines, beach obstacles, the slope of the beach, and buildings beyond it. The numbers correspond to other maps created for the invasion.

3
3
3
3
3
3
4
4

From left to right, Premier Stalin, President Roosevelt, and Prime Minister Churchill posed for photographers at their conference in Tehran, Iran.

the Soviets, Stalin might dissolve his uncomfortable alliance with the United Kingdom and America because the cost of life was just too steep.

The Allies needed to open that second front by capturing a port and flooding continental Europe with men and matériel. An amphibious invasion was a dangerous proposition, but it was their only option. The Allies had to throw everything into it and pray that it wouldn't all get heaved back into the sea. Their invasion plan needed to span not just multiple branches of the military but multiple branches of multiple countries' militaries. The matériel production, reconnaissance, training, bombardment, and troop movement had to be on a scale the world had never seen before, and everything needed to be done with the utmost secrecy.

SERIOUS MEETING

The Allies took a long time to decide where and when to invade as they intensely scrutinized their options in a number of high-powered meetings. In May 1943, Churchill and FDR met in Washington to discuss strategies for the war at the Trident Conference. America wanted to launch a large-scale invasion right away. Churchill, however, persuaded FDR that they should hold off for one year while they trained troops and amassed weapons, supplies, and, perhaps most importantly, landing craft. In the meantime, the Allies could invade Sicily and move up Italy, which would go a small way to creating the front in the west that Stalin needed.

In November, Churchill and Roosevelt met with Stalin in Tehran, Iran, to tell him the main invasion, code-named Operation Overlord, would come in the spring. Stalin demanded they name a commander for the operation to prove they were serious. Supreme Allied Commander Lieutenant General Sir Frederick E.

Morgan of the British Army had been working on the invasion plan for over a year, but the United States was committing the majority of the forces to the invasion. Therefore, the commander of Operation Overlord had to be an American. Roosevelt wanted to give Chief of Staff George Marshall the job. Marshall had assembled, trained, and equipped the US Army, so he deserved the chance to lead it. But Roosevelt also needed Marshall in Washington with him, and that need won out.

After days of deliberation, the job instead went to Dwight D. Eisenhower, then the Supreme Commander of the Allied Forces of the North African Theater of Operations (NATOUSA) and Allied Force Headquarters (AFHQ) in the Mediterranean. Far from a mere runner-up, Eisenhower was very qualified for the job. He had already led combined American and British forces in three successful invasions—Operation Torch in North Africa, Operation Husky in Sicily, and Operation Avalanche in mainland Italy—and he got along with the British far better than most American military men.

Eisenhower the Optimist

Dwight D. Eisenhower was born in Texas and raised in Kansas. This military leader and future president instilled confidence through his humanity and everyman persona. He believed that "without confidence, enthusiasm, and optimism in the command, victory is scarcely obtainable." That idea was put to the ultimate test during the planning of Operation Overlord. The week before the invasion, he wrote to his wife, Mamie, "I seem to live on a network of high tension wires." Despite the enormous personal stress and all the work involved in the planning—and the Brits' resistance to pretty much everything the Americans wanted to do—he still visited personally with the troops, talked with them, and assured them of victory.

PICKING THE PLACE

The Allies had to decide where to invade. They considered many places, from Holland to the Mediterranean coast, but it was hard

Omaha Beach today. The line of bluffs made this the toughest invasion beach, but it was also an essential location for the Allies if they wanted to get a foothold in Normandy.

to find a place that ticked all the boxes. The invasion site had to be near a port that wasn't too heavily defended. Its beaches couldn't be too steep for pack-laden troops, and the ground itself had to be able to support tremendously heavy vehicles and tanks. The beach also needed to have suitable exits. High cliffs with no roads on or off were not an option—they would be near impossible for troops to climb under enemy fire, and even if the men could scale them, the vehicles would be stuck, useless, on the beach. An acceptable landing site also had to be somewhat protected from the storms and swells of the Atlantic *and* close enough to southern England for the massive invasion forces to cross without detection. Finally, the site needed to be close to their real objective, the Rhine-Ruhr region of eastern Germany—the nation's industrial heartland. If the Allies could destroy the country's ability to make war, victory would soon follow.

Pas-de-Calais perfectly fit all the Allies' needs. This port city is located at the narrowest point in the English Channel between England and France, and from there an invading army can head straight east through Belgium into the Rhine-Ruhr region. Unfortunately for the Allies, the Germans also saw all these benefits and believed an invasion would almost certainly land there. They fortified Pas-de-Calais to the extreme, meaning the Allies had to find another place to land their forces. However, they needed the Germans to keep believing that they would invade at Pas-de-Calais so they could maintain some element of surprise.

After due consideration, the Allies chose the Calvados coast of Normandy, more through

This map, created by the US War Department, shows the length of the coastline considered for the invasion. Bayeux and Caen, toward the center, mark the stretch of beach the Allies eventually selected.

General Dwight D. Eisenhower joked with his men on a tour of the front in Salerno, Italy, in September 1943, just months before he was named commander of the Allied Expeditionary Forces.

elimination than preference. The Atlantic Wall was not as heavily fortified in Calvados as it was elsewhere. The city of Caen had a small airfield that the Allies thought they could capture without much difficulty. And Hitler's Ost battalions, far from his best fighting force, defended the area. These battalions were composed of soldiers taken prisoner from Eastern armies (Soviet, Ukrainian, Hungarian, Croatian, and even Indian and Korean) as well as from occupied countries (Poland, France, Italy, Norway). The Germans made the troops follow orders essentially at gunpoint, and the Ost troops were therefore often quick to abandon their posts or surrender.

The D in D-Day

Doom, defense, drop, disembarkation . . . many people think that the D in D-Day stands for something along these lines, but in fact it does not really stand for anything. It indicates the day on which an operation will be begin, so the closest thing it stands for is "day." (Similarly, H-Hour is the hour an operation will commence.) D-Day has become synonymous with the Allied invasion of Normandy, but it's a broadly used military term. D–1 is the day before an operation, and D+1 is the day after.

The chosen 50-mile stretch of Calvados coast had wide beaches without much of an incline. High bluffs lined some of it, but there weren't many vertical climbs. The Allies divided the assault area into five beaches: from west to east, Utah, Omaha, Gold, Juno, and Sword. These locations all had roads leading inland, which made suitable exits. The original plan had only four assault beaches, but when Eisenhower took over as commander of the Supreme Headquarters of the Allied Expeditionary Forces (SHAEF), he insisted on adding Utah. This western end of the attack would allow the Allies to eventually cut off the Cotentin Peninsula and capture the large port of Cherbourg.

THE BIG WEEK

The Allies did not wait for the invasion to get to work dismantling Germany's industrial war machine. From February 20 through 25, 1944, the Allies launched Operation Argument. Thousands of bombers and fighter planes assaulted industrial facilities in Germany that produced planes for the Luftwaffe. While the Allies lost more than 350 bombers and 28 fighters in the operation, the Germans lost even greater numbers of aircraft and pilots, and the attacks disrupted their means of producing replacements. "Big Week" gave the Allies the air supremacy they needed for an invasion.

SETTING THE DATE

With the location chosen, the Allies also had to decide on the equally important question of when to launch the invasion. The obvious answer was as soon as possible, but what really qualified as "possible"? Stormy March weather made the always turbulent English Channel too dangerous to cross. The US pushed for April, but the British said the weather would still be too unpredictable. They initially settled on the first suitable day after May 1, but when Eisenhower took over planning, he pushed that to June 1. The Allies needed more time to produce the crucial landing craft the invasion required—land ship, tank (LST); landing craft, tank (LCT);

B-26 Marauders dropped bombs on targets such as this railroad bridge in Rhineland-Palatinate, Germany, which disrupted the Reich's ability to get supplies into its occupied territories.

This 1870 painting by French artist Gustave Courbet shows waves crashing along the Normandy coast in the same kind of storm that postponed the D-Day operations for a full twenty-four hours.

landing craft, infantry (LCI); landing craft, medium (LCM); and landing craft, vehicle and personnel (LCVP). Without these, the troops quite simply couldn't get to the beaches. Churchill famously lamented that "the destinies of two great empires . . . seemed to be tied up in some god-damned things called LSTs."

The invasion force would have to cross the Channel at night, and planes and ships needed the light from at least a half-moon for navigation. The Germans were sure the Allies would come at high tide to minimize the amount of open beach the infantry would need to cross, but the Allies decided on a rising tide. That would allow the landing craft to reach the beach and then use the rising waters to back out. It also gave them a greater element of surprise.

The first window when the moon and the tides would be right was June 5 through 7, and indeed, the original date set for D-Day was June 5, 1944. While the Allies liberated Rome in southern

"THE QUESTION IS JUST HOW LONG CAN YOU HANG THIS OPERATION ON THE END OF A LIMB AND LET IT HANG THERE?" —GENERAL DWIGHT D. EISENHOWER

The Cross of Lorraine was the symbol of the French Free Forces and French Resistance during World War II. This memorial at Juno Beach marks where their leader, Charles de Gaulle, landed after D-Day.

Exercise Tiger

The Allies conducted a full-dress rehearsal with live ammunition on April 27 at Slapton Sands. Some of the landing craft were delayed during assault practice, but the bombardment force didn't get the message. As many as 110 men died from friendly fire. The training exercise went on anyway, as did communication problems. That afternoon, thousands of men boarded LSTs in Plymouth and Southampton, forming a convoy in Lyme Bay so they could storm Slapton Sands in a mock invasion of Utah Beach. Unfortunately, they had the wrong radio frequency for receiving information on real enemy activity. At 2:00 a.m. on April 28, while underway to Slapton, they missed a warning message that four E-boats (enemy boats) were in the Channel. The German *Schnellboote* fired their torpedoes at the LSTs, which had virtually no firepower or armor. The torpedoes hit LSTs 507, 531, and 289, and all but 289 sank. Captain John Doyle of the lead ship, LST 515, disobeyed orders and turned back to rescue 134 men. Unfortunately, 749 servicemen were killed during Exercise Tiger, more than twice the total casualties the Allies would suffer at the real Utah Beach. To make the disaster worse, the Germans realized the similarity between the Slapton Sands area and the eastern beaches of the Cotentin Peninsula. They then ramped up their efforts to reinforce their defenses in Normandy.

Europe on June 5, in the north, spring storms prevented them from launching the invasion, and they postponed the operation for one day. June 6's weather was still not ideal; the sky was overcast, and the Channel water was rough. But if the invasion force didn't go then, it would have to wait until the 19th, which would give the Nazis more time to fortify the coast and more opportunities to uncover the Allies' secret plan. As Eisenhower observed on the evening of June 4, as the SHAEF command weighed their options, "The question is, just how long can you hang this operation on the end of a limb and let it hang there?"

RECONNAISSANCE

Once the Allies had selected the invasion location, they endeavored to find out everything they could about it. By this point in the war, Allied air attacks on German soil had forced the Luftwaffe to concentrate its efforts on the defense of the Fatherland. The Allied Expeditionary Forces were therefore able to complete massive amounts of aerial reconnaissance

The commanders of the Allied Expeditionary Forces. From left to right: General Omar Bradley, commander of the 12th Army Group (American); Admiral Sir Bertram Ramsay, Allied naval commander (British); Air Chief Marshal and Deputy Supreme Commander Sir Arthur Tedder (British); Supreme Commander General Dwight Eisenhower (American); General Sir Bernard Montgomery, commander of the 21st Army Group (British); Air Vice Marshal Sir Trafford Leigh-Mallory (British); and General Walter Bedell Smith, Eisenhower's chief of staff (American).

photography on the French coast and inland defenses. Submarines undertook secret expeditions to Calvados, where men went onto the beaches under the cover of night and collected intelligence.

The French Resistance proved invaluable for reconnaissance, as its people were behind enemy lines and knew where the Germans focused on fortifying defenses. In fact, the French were forced to build the Atlantic Wall, so they knew it intimately. Getting information to Allied Command was challenging, but through word of mouth, radio transmissions, carrier pigeons, ingenuity, and personal sacrifice, the Resistance gave the Allies exact details about much of what the invasion force would face on D-Day.

FRENCH RESISTANCE

Being a part of the French Resistance, whose members were little armed, little organized, and little protected, was dangerous. People took enormous risks to get information to the Allies and carry out acts of sabotage, but these actions proved even more exacting and useful than the missions carried out by the Allies. If caught, members of the Resistance faced torture and even death, and not just for themselves but for their loved ones. They risked these retributions out of a sense of patriotism and the knowledge that even death was preferable to Nazi occupation. They destroyed train cars and bridges, took out lines of German communication, and blocked enemy movements. They sabotaged rail cars, which held up the best-outfitted Panzer division (an armored, mechanized, mobile infantry division), preventing the deadly Tiger tanks from quickly reaching the front. The Resistance therefore played a significant role in the ultimate success of D-Day and the ensuing invasion.

GETTING ALONG

Coordinating the logistics of D-Day was an epic feat. Men, matériel, transport, intelligence—all the elements of the invasion had to be understood, amassed, and made to work together. Operations that span multiple branches of the military often face challenges in leadership.

The navy wants one thing, the air force another, and the army something else. They all want the best resources, and they want plans to benefit their own men. Planning the Normandy invasion faced that problem on an international level, as America, the UK, Canada, and Free France (the exiled French government and military led by Charles de Gaulle) tried to work together. Eisenhower didn't personally like the British Army commander, General Bernard Law Montgomery—he was concerned that Montgomery and Air Vice Marshal Sir Trafford Leigh-Mallory were too cautious for the job at hand. Regardless, he needed them, so he resolved to get the best out of them. But they had to know who was in charge.

At the outset of planning Operation Overlord, Eisenhower threatened to "request relief" from his post if he wasn't given command over both the British and American air forces to conduct his Transportation Plan. He felt the strategic bombing of key targets in France to reduce Germany's ability to move its forces around the country in the months leading up to the invasion was crucial. Churchill and other commanders, on the other hand, believed that plan would cause too many civilian casualties. They consulted the French, who accepted the danger. Ultimately Churchill, the Allied War Cabinet, and President Roosevelt signed off on the Transportation Plan, which ended up playing a large role in the ultimate success of Operation Overlord.

Eisenhower faced arguments like this one over and over again. Practically every decision that needed to be made met opposition from one quarter or another, but Eisenhower remained indefatigable, informed, and resolute.

THE PLAN

Eisenhower told General Omar Bradley, commander of the US First Army, "This operation is not being

This map shows the broad details of the Allies' invasion plan. The US Airborne and Army came in on the west, while the British and Canadians took the east.

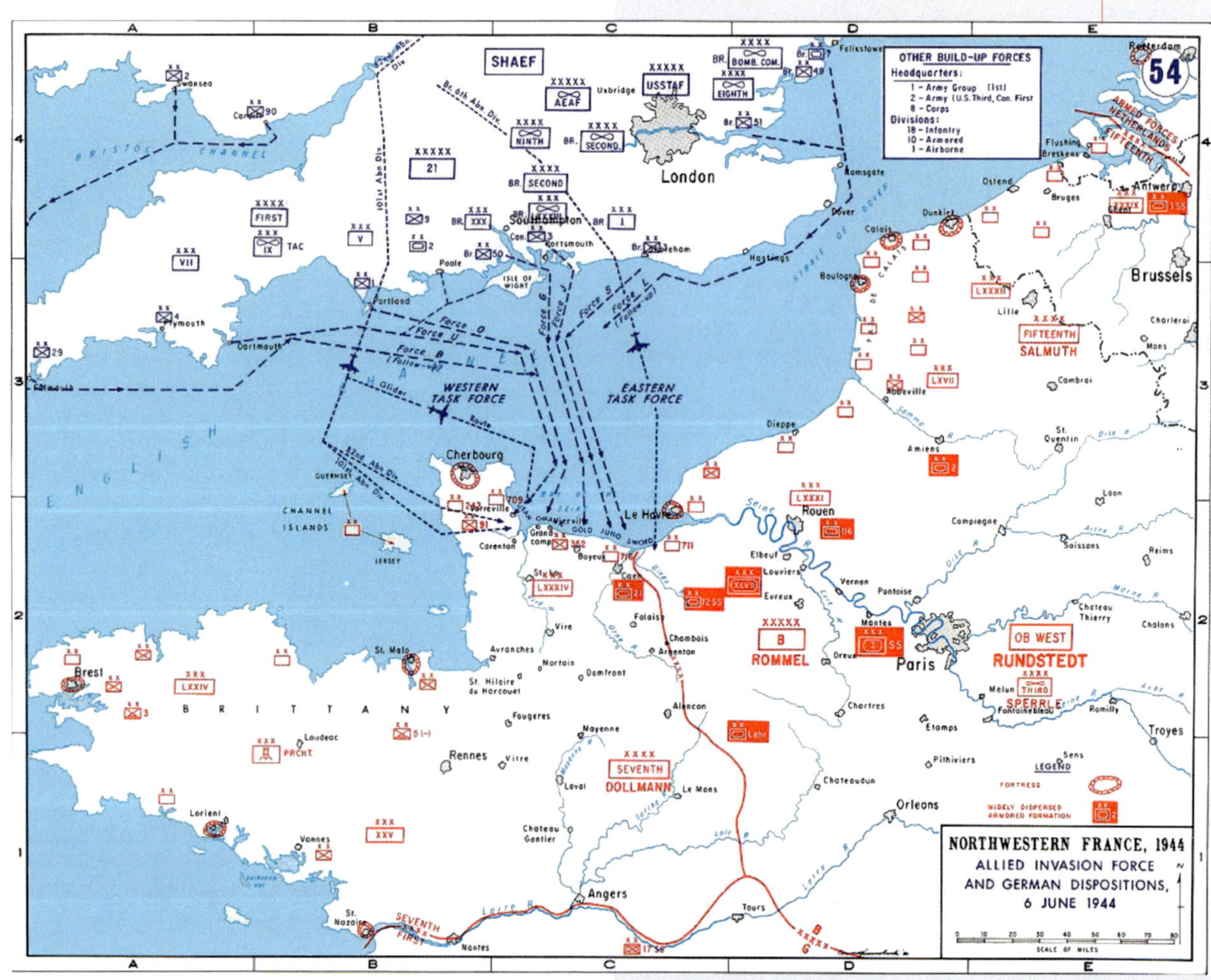

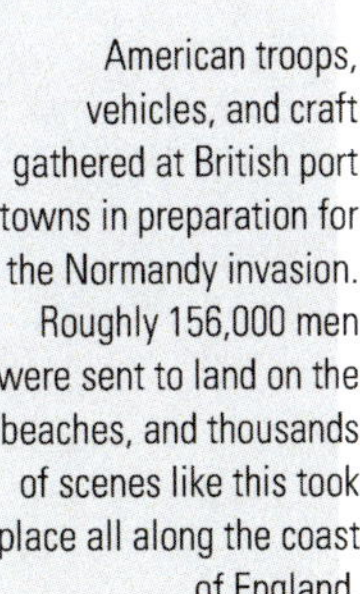

American troops, vehicles, and craft gathered at British port towns in preparation for the Normandy invasion. Roughly 156,000 men were sent to land on the beaches, and thousands of scenes like this took place all along the coast of England.

planned with any alternatives. This operation is planned as a victory, and that's the way it's going to be. We're going down there, and we're throwing everything we have into it, and we're going to make it a success." On April 7, the high command presented the outline of the plan to the commanders of the divisions who would be participating in the invasion. With their objectives in hand, the commanders composed detailed plans from the battalion level down to individual boat teams. They would tweak the particulars until the moment the invasion was launched, but the main points were set.

The US First Army would invade the western beaches, Utah and Omaha. The British Second Army would take the eastern beaches, Gold, Juno, and Sword, though Canadian infantry would actually conduct the Juno landings under the command of the British Army. An aerial assault of the entire area would begin shortly after midnight. Airborne troops from the British 6th Airborne Division would knock out the battery at Merville and the bridge over the Dives river. They would also capture the bridges over the Orne river and its canal. The US 101st Airborne would secure the raised causeways through the fields behind Utah Beach, which the Nazis had flooded to further fortify the area's defenses. The 82nd Airborne would block enemy reinforcements from entering the Cotentin Peninsula in the west. The paratroopers and glider-borne troops from all the divisions would then provide cover on the east and west flanks of the invasion.

At dawn, the Allies would launch a naval and air bombardment to take out beach batteries and inland defenses as well as create craters that would serve as foxholes for the ground troops. Minutes before the ground assault, LCTs variously outfitted with rocket launchers and artillery would take out any defenses left standing on the beaches.

Just after the LCTs arrived, the first waves of infantry would land, followed quickly by combat engineers charged with destroying any mines and obstacles standing between the water and the beach exits. Then more infantrymen, more engineers, more vehicles, and more supplies would come in wave after wave. Heavy artillery would come ashore by H+3 (three hours after the start of the battle), the beaches would be cleared and the exits secured, and trucks and salvage companies would move in.

The commanders planned for every man, minute, and meter of beach. The plan was so meticulous that when infantrymen were briefed, some felt like nothing could go wrong. Others thought the hundreds of pages of plans would go right out the window the moment the fighting started and the only plan worth anything was to just get off the beach.

"THROWING YOURSELF ACROSS THE BUNK YOU SAID—'COMBAT CAN'T BE THAT ROUGH!'"

—SCRAPBOOK FROM THE 506TH PARACHUTE INFANTRY REGIMENT

The US Coast Guard trained for the beach invasion with landing craft, infantry (LCI) at Slapton Sands, which was topographically similar to Utah Beach and replicated the obstacles there.

Even Eisenhower quoted a phrase he had learned in the army, "Before the battle plans are everything, but as soon as battle is joined plans are worthless."

Roughly 156,000 troops, 7,000 vessels, and 12,000 aircraft were heading across the Channel, so a finely tuned plan was essential just to avoid a deadly traffic jam. Reluctant as Churchill was, when he described the plan to Parliament on D-Day itself, he would exclaim, "What a plan!"

TRAINING

Much of the pre-invasion army training was getting to and across the beaches, which would require taking out the concrete pillboxes and batteries defending them. These fortifications were the backbone of the Atlantic Wall. American troops began their training in the US, and when they traded the sunshine of the American South for the gloomy weather of Southern England, they felt demoralized. The food was terrible, and many members of the 29th Infantry Division felt like lab rats during the grueling exercises used to test tactics being developed for the invasion.

The Allies re-created the Normandy fortifications down to the pillbox at training facilities such as Inverness, Scotland, which replicated Juno Beach, and Slapton Sands in Devon, England, which mimicked Utah. Even if everything went to hell when troops got to the beach, they would be familiar with the landscape and what they needed to do there.

The men marched, loaded and unloaded craft, slept in foxholes, and belly-crawled under barbed wire as live rounds shot over their heads. They practiced on the firing range, practiced on the landing craft, and practiced on the beaches. They ran obstacle courses, rehearsed demolishing obstacles, and did company and battalion exercises, all while those in charge tested, eliminated, and perfected their tactics.

As hard as infantry training was, airborne troops had it even tougher. All but the glider units were volunteers, and they started three-day training exercises with a jump, carrying full packs. They marched for over 100 miles and inevitably started to believe that no battle could be that bad. According to a scrapbook from the 506th Parachute Infantry Regiment, "You finally dragged your weary body those last few torturous kilometers, and throwing yourself across the bunk you said—'Combat can't be that rough!'" Sadly, they were wrong. ■

DECEPTION PLANS

Operation Fortitude

The success of Operation Overlord relied heavily on the element of surprise, so the Allies organized Operation Fortitude, an elaborate web of deception to mislead the Wehrmacht as to the where and when of the invasion. Fortitude itself was just one component of the Allies' massive misinformation campaign for the Normandy landings, collectively code-named Operation Bodyguard.

The Allies divided Operation Fortitude into Fortitude North, designed to deceive the Germans into thinking an invasion force was coming to Norway, and Fortitude South, which would perpetuate the Pas-de-Calais ruse. Both used the Double Cross System, a network of German spies that the British had turned into double agents, essentially at gunpoint. The Reich trusted these operatives, who fed them just enough truth mixed in with lies to make the Germans fall for the deception.

Fortitude North was based in Scotland, from which the Allies launched raids and "secret" missions to Norway to collect soil samples and other recon. Seeing this, Hitler positioned thirteen divisions—averaging 15,000 men each—as well as 90,000 personnel from the navy, 60,000 from the air force, 6,000 from the SS (for *Schutzstaffel*, meaning "Protection Echelon"), and 12,000 from the paramilitary in Norway, Denmark, and Finland. Together, that was about 365,000 men he couldn't position in Normandy.

Fortitude South operated out of Kent, just across the Channel from Pas-de-Calais, and was far bigger than its northern brother. The famed Lieutenant General George S. Patton, who the Germans assumed would lead the invasion, was put in command of the First US Army Group (FUSAG). This force was largely fictitious, consisting mostly of dummy wooden aircraft, fake landing craft, inflatable tanks, mock buildings, and camps set up to make the Germans believe resources were being concentrated in Kent. Aerial recon the Nazis conducted even showed Patton visiting his "troops."

To further the deception, a blizzard of radio traffic emanated daily from the region, simulating the communications activities one might expect of an entire army group. By mixing real information with false in the transmissions, the Allies were able to fool the Germans into thinking that a vast invasion force was assembling in Kent to land in Calais.

Additionally, unbeknownst to the Germans, the Allies had long since cracked the secret to the Germans' Enigma cipher machines, which created supposedly unbreakable codes. The Allies could now read the Germans' coded messages at will, and from these so-called "Ultra" decrypts, they knew their plans of deception were working. General Rommel thought the invasion wouldn't happen until June 20, and Hitler openly wondered whether it would come at all. Operation Fortitude worked so well overall that for days after D-Day, the Germans thought the Normandy invasion was a feint and remained braced for a "real" invasion at Pas-de-Calais.

Inflatable tanks, like this one, as well as dummy planes, landing craft, and even infantry camps, fooled the Germans into thinking the Allies were far better equipped for an invasion than they actually were.

CROSSING THE CHANNEL

The Allies were ready to throw everything they had at Germany's Atlantic Wall. If their plan failed, the war would continue to grind on.

After years of planning, training, and amassing supplies, the moment had come for the Allies to launch their staggering amount of manpower and matériel over the rough June waters of the English Channel. Roughly 5,000 vessels and 156,000 Allied troops participated in Operation Neptune, the code name for the stage of Operation Overlord that involved crossing the Channel and the landing operations in Normandy. Getting that many craft across the water was remarkable in itself, but the operation was exponentially more complex than just the physical crossing. The Allies had to first marshal and load 133,000 landing troops along with the weapons, vehicles, and supplies they would need to storm five landing sites over 50 miles of Normandy coastline. The armada it took to accomplish this was so massive that ships stretched out to the water's horizon in all directions as they crossed the Channel.

The thousands of craft that took part in this operation ranged from armored warships with enormous firepower that would bombard the German defenses to small, minimally-armed infantry landing

The USS *Tide* was one of the minesweepers that led the invasion. On June 7, it hit a mine and sank. This photo was taken shortly before it went down, as PT-509 and the USS *Pheasant* stood by to pick up survivors.

craft that held just thirty men each. The American, British, French, Canadian, Norwegian, Polish, Greek, and Dutch Navies provided the battleships, destroyers, escorts, heavy and light cruisers, transports, gunboats, and legions of landing craft that cruised the choppy waters the night of June 5.

FIRST, THE MINESWEEPERS

The success of Operation Neptune rested on many shoulders, all pivotally important. Before the armada made its way from England to France, the minesweepers made the crossing to clear the way. First, they cleared a wide lane from the Isle of Wight to "Point Z." The warships from all the ports converged at this point, nicknamed Piccadilly Circus, to form the five convoys headed for the five different beaches. Once across the Channel, fleet minesweeping flotillas cleared two lanes of approach for each beach. Near shore, they swept an area clear for the warships to bombard the coastal defenses. They finished their work at 0303 on June 6, just six minutes before German radar spotted the fleet. If the minesweepers had not been so deft, the invasion would not have been so successful.

LCTS AND HOBART'S FUNNIES

The LCT flotillas came next, carrying vehicles (tanks and jeeps) with their crews, weapons, and supplies. Each LCT was 120 to 192 feet long (depending on the model) and had two 20-millimeter cannons. A flat bottom and shallow draft allowed them to pass over obstacles, but they had a hard time staying on course in strong tides or heavy winds—both of which were virtually omnipresent in the English Channel in June.

A typical LCT carried four "swimming" Duplex Drive (DD) tanks as well as four jeeps with trailers of ammunition and the crews for the tanks and jeeps. The DD tanks were just one of the assault-vehicle innovations General Percy Hobart had designed. Hobart and his team came up with a wide range of modifications to deal with the issues that standard Churchill and Sherman tanks faced in World War II. The designs became known as "Hobart's Funnies," and several of these mods were famously used in the Normandy invasion.

A DD tank "swam" thanks to a waterproof canvas screen that inflated around it, allowing it to float to the shore, where it could shed its flotation device. The tank's main engine powered twin propellers

Ships gathered at Piccadilly Circus as they prepared to cross the English Channel for the D-Day invasion. The lines of craft, large and small, spread out to the horizon.

LCT 495 (foreground) towed a barrage balloon past the HMS *John Booker* during a rehearsal for the Normandy invasion. She also had trucks and even a canoe on deck.

that drove them in the water. This "Duplex Drive" gave them their "DD" nickname, which led troops to call them "Donald Duck tanks."

The invasion fleet also carried Crabs, Sherman tanks with rotating drums of chains used to explode mines in their path. Each Crab also came equipped with a box-girder bridge that crews could lay across antitank ditches.

With these mobility upgrades, troops could take tanks to more places and travel farther than before. Unfortunately, the DD tanks, which were supposed to land five minutes before H-Hour to provide cover for the infantry, did not work as hoped during the beach landings at Normandy.

This photo of an LCT on the deck of an LST gives a clear view of the former's flat bottom and its ramp used to discharge tanks.

THE BOMBARDMENT GROUP

The firepower was up next in the armada: battleships, cruisers, and destroyers. The American battleships USS *Arkansas* and *Texas* headed to Omaha. The *Nevada* went to Utah, and the British HMS *Ramillies*, *Rodney*, and *Warspite* anchored off Sword (the *Nelson* was held in reserve). None of these ships were new. The *Rodney* and the *Nelson*, commissioned in 1927, were the newest, and the rest had been commissioned in the 1910s. Old as they were, however, the battleships had big guns of 12, 14, 15, and 16 inches that could face off against the Germans' beach guns, which ranged from 75 to 170 millimeters (roughly 3 to 7 inches), and their bigger inland batteries, which went up to 210 millimeters (about 8 inches).

Twenty light cruisers, five heavy cruisers, and 36 destroyers rounded out the bombardment group. The battleships and cruisers took the lead with the destroyers following. Transports and larger ships followed, arriving at their transport sectors by 0400. At 0510, these craft moved in to their launch positions about 3 miles from shore; 12 minutes later, at 0522, the crews went to their beaching stations. Despite the rough waters, the beaches seemed to be asleep. Lieutenant Ross Olsen of the *Nevada* recalled, "We felt like we were sneaking up on the enemy and even talked in whispers, thinking we might be heard by the Germans on the beach, which of course was impossible."

TRANSPORTS AND LANDING CRAFT

Three troop transport ships were used for the American side of the invasion: the USS *Samuel Chase* and *Charles Carroll* (both heading to Omaha) and the USS *Bayfield* (the flagship for Utah). They carried troops across the Channel and brought them to the landing craft that would take them to the beaches. After the assault began, those same craft took wounded men back to the carriers.

LSTs (landing ship, tanks) carried not just tanks but also LCCs (landing craft, control), which were crew-only boats that served as traffic control for the other landing craft. Lieutenant Howard Vander Beek, commander of LCC 60, recalled that they "felt naked, defenseless. Although hundreds of friendly guns on US battleships, cruisers, and destroyers behind us were poised and silent, ready to begin their onslaught, there were Wehrmacht batteries ahead, waiting for enough light to fire."

LSTs used davits to lower craft into the sea, but they also had ramps

The battleships USS *Nevada* and *Texas*. The *Nevada* (lead ship) was the only battleship to get underway at Pearl Harbor. It was almost destroyed there, but massive salvage efforts repaired the ship, which took part in not only the D-Day invasion but also the atomic bomb tests at Bikini Atoll.

What of the Weather?

The odds that the weather would be suitable during the launch windows of June 5–7 and 19–20 were thirteen to one against, according to the meteorologists working on the plan. D-Day was initially set for June 5, but just two hours before the ships were to sail, Eisenhower decided to stall for one day at the insistence of the meteorological teams of the British Royal Air Force and Royal Navy. The US meteorological team had wanted to go, but the Brits proved them wrong when a storm swept through the Channel.

As June 6 approached, the RAF still said the conditions were a "no-go," but the Navy and US team approved the launch anyway. The weather was suitable, but just barely. Stiff winds and a thick cloud cover were not ideal, but the bad weather further secured the element of surprise. The Germans didn't think the Allies would—or could—invade in such foul conditions.

to launch amphibious landing craft such as DUKWs—amphibious trucks that weighed 2.5 tons each. The LSTs' work didn't end there. They also towed "Rhino ferries" of heavy equipment and vehicles. These Rhinos had their own outboard propulsion to run them onto the beaches, as LSTs could not come all the way to shore.

The Allies used 229 LSTs carrying 1,089 LCVPs on D-Day, but there were plenty of other self-propelled landing craft on hand, including 245 LCIs (infantry), 481 LCMs (medium), and 911 LCTs. These landing craft lined up in columns that stretched from the Isle of Wight to Normandy in such close proximity that the fact they bumped but never crashed is nothing short of astonishing. Also amazing is that they were on the water for over four hours before being picked up on German radar thanks to Allied bombers that dropped foil strips, code-named "Windows," which caused echoes in the German radar systems.

Though the crossing was absolutely a success, not everything went wonderfully to plan. One challenge was the way troops had to board some landing craft, by

A Sherman tank disembarked an LST and rolled ashore in Bradford, Virginia, during training operations. The weather and waves here were more cooperative than they were in Southern England.

"WE FELT LIKE WE WERE SNEAKING UP ON THE ENEMY AND EVEN TALKED IN WHISPERS, THINKING WE MIGHT BE HEARD." —LIEUTENANT ROSS OLSEN

This 1941 Higgins boat demonstrated its ability to carry and land a truck on a beach. This was the model used for the invasion's LCVPs.

climbing down nets from the sides of LSTs. Commanding officers tried to give men the order to jump the final distance from the net to the boat at the top of a swell, but they had a hard time getting the timing right. Even before the first wave of infantry was fully loaded onto the landing craft, some had broken bones, and a few were crushed to death between their boats and the LSTs.

HIGGINS BOATS

The Higgins boat—formally called landing craft, vehicle and personnel (LCVP)—was perhaps the most critical landing craft at D-Day. Designed by Andrew Higgins of New Orleans, Louisiana, this flat-bottomed craft was essentially a barge, typically made of plywood and armed with just two Browning machine guns. At 36 feet long and 11 feet wide, a Higgins boat could carry thirty-six fully equipped men but often transported a dozen men and a jeep. A shallow draft of only about 3 feet allowed it to safely pass over underwater mines and obstacles, but the boat was still highly maneuverable. It could pull up to a beach, discharge its men down a metal ramp in a matter of seconds, and then whip around to go pick up another transport load.

Some 23,000 of these boats were built by Higgins Industries, but that didn't happen without some controversy. Andrew Higgins had a bad whiskey habit and a temperament that matched. He said the US Navy didn't "know one damn thing about small boats," which did not endear him to Navy officials. The navy had required the LCVPs to be 30 feet, but Higgins insisted they be 36. But Operation Overlord spanned many branches of the military, and once the Marines saw what Higgins's boats could do (after years of frustration with the Navy Bureau of Ships failing to design a landing craft that would serve the Marines' needs), he landed the contract to make the boats his way. At peak production, he employed roughly thirty thousand people without a thought to race or gender. His workforce made the boats that made the invasion possible. In a 1964 interview, Eisenhower told historian Stephen Ambrose that Andrew Higgins was "the man who won the war for us." ■

Seasickness

Many of the soldiers who landed on D-Day had already been aboard their transport ships for days in bad weather. Seasickness was rampant on those vessels, which meant that as H-Hour approached, the men were running more on adrenaline than calories. There wasn't even room to sit on the LCVPs, so everyone had to stand, crowded and burdened by the weight of their packs and weapons. As the boats pitched around in the rough waters, bobbing and dropping, the Americans lost their breakfasts of Spam and coffee while the Brits lost their eggs and rum. Waves broke over the gunwales, soaking the men. The conditions on the landing craft were so abysmal that men jumped over the sides as soon as they got close enough to shore, feeling like no matter what the Germans threw at them, it couldn't be as bad as the damn boats.

GERMAN DEFENSES

The Atlantic Wall

Hitler knew the Allied forces would eventually storm Festung Europa, or Fortress Europe, the name both sides used for the Nazi-occupied territories in continental Europe. For the Reich to endure an invasion, its forces would have to stop it at the beaches and fling the invaders back into the sea. So on March 23, 1942, Hitler issued Directive No. 40, the basic plan for the Atlantic Wall—a 2,000-mile-long network of fixed fortifications stretching from the northern tip of Norway down to the Franco-Spanish border.

For two years, the Nazis built this line of concrete and steel defenses in the countries they occupied along the Atlantic, though they forced the occupied citizenry to do the actual construction work. Billions of reichsmarks went into 1.2 million tons of steel and 17 million cubic meters of concrete to create fortresses at key cities and ports, install batteries of big guns, and station troops along the length of the wall.

In early 1944, as the odds of an Allied invasion increased by the day, General Erwin Rommel was put in charge of improving the wall's defenses. After his first inspection of the wall, he deemed what he saw a farce. He ordered hundreds of heavily armed pillboxes be built, miles of barbed wire strung, and literally millions of mines sunk, buried, and hidden to blast ships, infantry, paratroopers, tanks, and anything else the Allies could throw at them. Along the Normandy coast, millions of mines peppered the beaches and intertidal zones. He planted fields of "Rommel's asparagus"—sharpened poles that would snag or impale paratroopers and break up gliders—anywhere he thought would be a good landing spot. He angled gun bunkers to shoot across beaches instead of into the water, so that as infantry struggled onto the sand, they'd be caught in a vicious web of crossfire just as they were most vulnerable.

While Rommel did manage to make a formidable war machine to repel an invasion force, it was spread thin. The Allies knew the landing zones they'd picked didn't have the heaviest fortifications. While many men fell to these stationary defenses on D-Day, the Atlantic Wall proved to be no match for the waves and waves of Allied troops who stormed the beaches.

The Atlantic Wall stretched from the northernmost part of Norway down to the border between France and Spain, covering the northern European coast that was under German occupation.

THE WEE HOURS

In the dark morning hours, airborne troops dropped into France by the thousands with only antiaircraft fire to light their way.

As the naval convoys made their way across the English Channel in the dark early hours of June 6, the air assault began. Nearly 1,000 Allied planes took off at 0000, and over the course of the day 12,000 aircraft flew nearly 15,000 sorties. They dropped countless bombs, as 15,500 Americans parachuted in, 7,900 British paratroopers made their jumps, and 4,000 glider troops faced flooded fields and Rommel's asparagus. And they did it all in windy conditions, under a cloud cover that was nearly blinding. Despite the treacherous weather, these airborne troops would take out German defenses, capture tactically crucial locations, and confuse the enemy about the true nature of the invasion.

To that end, "Ruperts" were the first Allies to land in France—dummy paratroopers made of burlap and equipped with explosives, noisemakers, and foil Windows. When Ruperts landed, their explosives burned them up so that the enemy soldiers who found them could not quickly detect the deception.

Two hundred Ruperts dropped around the Seine, leading a German

SHAEF Commander Dwight D. Eisenhower told paratroopers of the 502nd Parachute Infantry Regiment that their orders were "full victory—nothing else."

23

commander to think a massive invasion was coming near Le Havre, far north of the real landing zones. Another 200 dummies dropped southwest of Caen, along with two teams of British Special Air Service men. When the SAS teams landed, they used gramophones to play a recording of soldiers shouting and setting off bombs. Some 2,000 Germans were drawn away from the beaches and into the woods to look for a large force of men who weren't there.

The SAS teams were supposed to meet up with American troops after nine days, but one team ended up spending six weeks on the run behind enemy lines until they were captured after a shootout in a barn. At the outset of the mission, none of them expected to survive, but miraculously, they all did. When France was liberated, they regained their freedom. Eight other SAS team members were lost, killed either in France or at the Bergen-Belsen concentration camp.

PATHFINDERS

At 0010 the "pathfinders" of the 101st Airborne were the first wave of live parachutists to make their jumps. One minute later, German troops detected them. On the ground, the pathfinders had to mark drop zones for the thousands of paratroopers who were scheduled to drop 30 minutes later. They marked the zones using a "Eureka" radar beacon, a short-range radio navigation system that would transmit a signal to a "Rebecca" receiver on the lead C-47s. But that wasn't as easy as it might sound. The receiving Rebecca had to be within 2 miles of the Eureka to pick up the signal, and the Eureka itself was 65 pounds of additional weight for the man who carried it. The Eureka also could only guide the Rebecca to the general area, so the pathfinders set out Holophane lights on the ground in a T shape to alert pilots to the precise drop locations. Unfortunately, the D-Day pathfinders weren't able to set out most of their drop-zone markers as planned.

The second group of pathfinders, from the 22nd Independent Parachute Company, jumped from 0020 to 0035, and the third, from the 82nd Airborne, jumped at 0121 and 0138. Sergeant Elmo Jones of the 505th Parachute Infantry Regiment in the first pathfinder wave later recalled, "The first thing

Paratroopers from the 101st Airborne descended toward the many dangers behind Utah Beach during the wee hours of the invasion.

Pathfinders from the British 6th Airborne Division synchronized their watches as they prepared to head over the Channel and mark landing zones.

The original Pegasus Bridge ("Ham"), which was taken by the British Airborne at the very start of D-Day, has been replaced, but the original, shown here, was moved to Lower Normandy and stands as a monument to its liberators.

I thought, without even trying to get out of my parachute, was, *Damn, I just cracked the Atlantic Wall.*"

Antiaircraft fire drove the pathfinders' Albemarle transport planes off course, and a thick cloud bank forced the men to jump from too high or low an altitude. Of the 18 teams of pathfinders that went out, only one landed at its target, meaning they were only able to accurately mark one of the six drop zones. Because all aircraft were on radio silence, the pilots couldn't warn others about the cloud bank or tell anyone that most of the pathfinders hadn't been able to mark their drop zones.

HAM AND JAM

D Company from the British 6th Airborne Division was the first unit to go into action on D-Day. The men's mission was code-named Operation Deadstick. At 0016, Horsa gliders dropped above Cabourg and landed exactly where they were supposed to: beside the Bénouville Bridge that spanned the Caen Canal (code-named Ham) and the Ranville Bridge over the Orne (code-named Jam). In under 15 minutes, D Company secured the bridges, the only eastward exits for Sword Beach, and sent out a "Ham and Jam" victory message over the radio. The French later renamed the "Ham" bridge over the canal the Pegasus Bridge for the emblem of the British airborne, and they renamed "Jam" Horsa Bridge in honor of the gliders. Not all glider missions would go so inspiringly well.

OVER THE COTENTIN PENINSULA

Thirteen thousand American paratroopers from the 82nd and 101st Airborne jumped over the Cotentin Peninsula to support the western American beaches in Missions Albany and Boston. They made the crossing in C-47 Skytrains that were designed for cargo and passengers—not for combat. These craft didn't have armor or guns. Many of the pilots had never flown combat missions before, nor were they adept at night flying. Despite all this, in the still-dark morning hours an enormous armada of over 800 C-47s flew for two-plus hours in total radio silence over the Channel and into enemy airspace. Twenty serials of 36, 45, or 54 aircraft stretched out for over 300 miles with only 100 feet between each plane. They flew low to avoid radar detection, then swooped high to dodge antiaircraft defenses, then dove again to get to the jump altitude.

Despite the planes facing defensive fire as they approached the peninsula, all went well until they encountered the cloud bank that had caused so much confusion for the pathfinders. The C-47s scattered

"THE FIRST THING I THOUGHT . . . *I JUST CRACKED THE ATLANTIC WALL.*" —SERGEANT ELMO JONES

to avoid colliding with one another, and when they emerged from the clouds, German fire bombarded them. Searchlights swept the sky, and tracers whizzed through the air. Despite all the flak thrown at them, the Allies lost only 46 planes.

The drop zones were either unmarked or in the wrong places, but the pilots hardly knew where they were anyway. The paratroopers were supposed to jump from 600 feet at 90 miles per hour, but instead they jumped from anywhere between 300 and 2,000 feet at speeds of up to 150 miles per hour. Meanwhile, planes were hit by enemy fire, exploding and dropping out of the sky all around. Private Dwayne Burns of the 508th Parachute Infantry Regiment recalled he "could hear the machine-gun rounds walking across the wings. . . . Of all the training we had, there was not anything that had prepared us for this."

The one blessing in disguise was that because the paratroopers couldn't see the ground, they couldn't tense up before they hit it. This decreased but by no means eliminated injuries. And sadly, it was no help for the men who landed in the flooded fields and drowned.

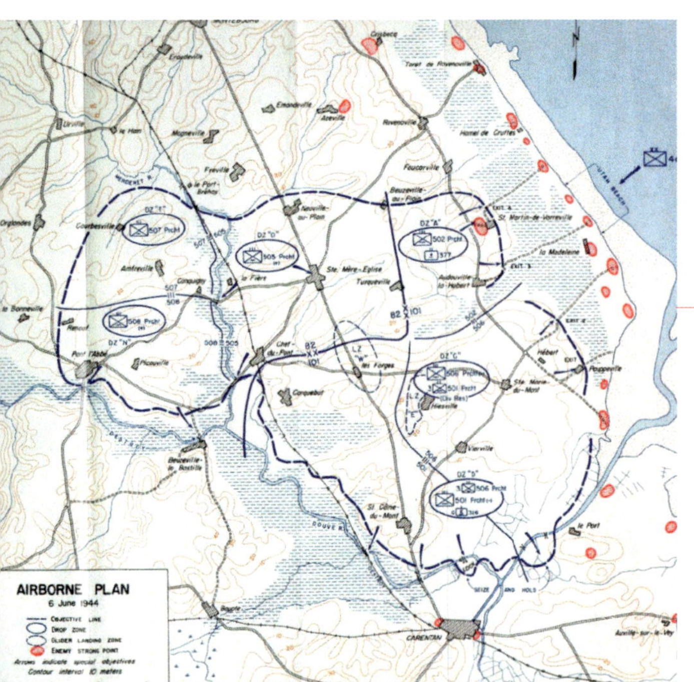

The solid circles show the intended landing zones for the paratrooper infantry regiments on D-Day. The dash-line circles show the glider landing zones.

MISSION ALBANY

The 6,600 paratroopers in the first wave of the 101st Airborne were known as the Screaming Eagles. They jumped between 0048 and 0140, trying to hit drop zones A, C, and D, but they were badly scattered. Only 1,100 paratroopers landed in their target drop zones, while 1,500 dropped so far outside their intended zones that they were captured or killed. No matter where the paratroopers landed, once on the ground, they did their best to achieve the objectives of Mission Albany. They needed to secure four causeway exits behind Utah Beach and capture the battery at Saint-Martin-de-Varreville, two footbridges, and the locks that had allowed the Germans to flood the fields. They were also charged with destroying several bridges and securing a position of attack, all while fighting the Germans on the ground and putting up roadblocks to cut off the enemy from the beach.

The 502nd Parachute Infantry Regiment (PIR), though scattered and far from their intended drop zone, DZ A, accomplished its objectives. But it was bittersweet. The Germans had already deserted the battery at Varreville and removed its guns, so the Allied troops took it easily. They captured their two target exits from the beach, but one was too close to

The Airborne Divisions

Major Generals Maxwell D. Taylor and Matthew B. Ridgway commanded the American 101st and 82nd Airborne Divisions, respectively. A total of 15,500 airborne troops supported Utah Beach to the west, while 7,900 troops from the British 6th Airborne Division, commanded by Major General Richard Nelson Gale, backed up Sword Beach on the east flank. To avoid flying over the naval convoys, which would allow the Germans to detect the fleet, the pilots flew in from the west, over the Cotentin Peninsula.

Paratroopers from the 101st as they awaited takeoff. The man in the foreground held Eisenhower's Order of the Day and a bazooka.

active German batteries to be of any use. And some of the troops were stuck in a maze of hedgerows and spent the day just trying to regroup.

The second wave of C-47s carrying the 506th PIR scattered in the clouds and flak, but the 1st Battalion still landed in its drop zone, DZ C. The 2nd, however, landed too far north and ended up in the same area as some of the 501st PIR. They combined forces and worked to take the causeways behind Utah. The 3rd Battalion of the 501st was also supposed to land in DZ C to secure an area near Hiesville for incoming gliders to land, but they were badly scattered. Major General Taylor instead rallied what men he could find to secure Exit 1 under command of Lieutenant Colonel Julian Ewell. It took them four hours of fighting Germans from house to house, which resulted in about 50 percent casualties, but they made it.

Despite flak, searchlights, and six downed C-47s, most of the men from the third wave (composed of men from both the 501st and 506th) landed near their target, DZ D. Unfortunately, since they were the third wave and the DZ was an obvious landing choice, the Germans were waiting for them. The Allies suffered heavy casualties and lost senior officers. While they didn't achieve their objective of destroying a highway bridge, they did capture the lock at La Barquette at 0400 and seize two footbridges at 0430.

MISSION BOSTON

The "All American" 82nd Airborne Division was on Mission Boston: land two regiments in drop zones T and N, west of the Merderet river, and one in DZ O, east of it. There, they had to destroy two bridges, secure a bridgehead on the west bank, and capture the town of Sainte-Mère-Église. Divided into three forces—A, B, and C—they began their drops at 0151 and continued to jump until 0244.

The 505th Parachute Infantry Regiment was a veteran regiment and so was given the most dangerous missions, which were in DZ O. Their C-47s stayed in formation, flying over the cloud bank instead of scattering inside it. The pathfinders had been able to mark DZ O, so most of the paratroopers jumped where they were meant to and landed where they were meant to. Their success continued, and they accomplished most of their first objectives pretty much on schedule. The 3rd Battalion captured Sainte-Mère-Église, and the 2nd took up a defensive position north of the town. German counterattacks on Sainte-Mère-Église came later in the day, and the 2nd suffered heavy casualties, but their defenses held.

This Handley Page Halifax heavy bomber of the British Royal Air Force took off for Normandy towing a Horsa glider. Gliders were nicknamed "tow targets" and "flying coffins" because they had no power of their own and often crashed or were shot down.

The 1st Battalion was charged with securing the bridge over the Merderet at La Fière from the east. As the paratroopers approached the bridge, they faced off with German troops and entrenched machine-gun teams. The Germans repulsed them over and over. They finally made it across the bridge around 1200, only for the Germans to retake the bridge an hour later. By most accounts, the defenses at the bridge at Chef-du-Pont were just as formidable, and neither bridge was captured on D-Day. Bitter fighting lasted in the area for four days before the Allies finally had their decisive victory.

While the 505th PIR had some of the most successful drops of the day, the 508th, which had never seen combat before, had the worst. Its C-47s scattered in the clouds, only to emerge under heavy fire with no signs of the pathfinders' beacons in sight. Half the regiment dropped, scattered far and wide in a valley the Allies hadn't realized was flooded. Lieutenant Ralph DeWeese landed in that water. Later, he recalled, "Several times I thought it was no use and decided to open my mouth and drown, but each time the wind would slack up enough for me to put my head out of the water and catch a breath." Most of the men of the 508th couldn't even get to their D-Day objectives.

The troops of the 507th also landed scattered from their target, the west approach to the bridge at La Fière. While some of them made it to the bridge to fight, others struggled to regroup, finding themselves in skirmishes miles inland. Others landed in the same area as the 101st Airborne and temporarily joined up with that division.

GLIDER REINFORCEMENTS

After the paratroopers made their jumps, glider-borne aircraft went in as reinforcements. C-47s towed the gliders on 300-yard-long nylon ropes. These largely wooden craft carried troops, jeeps, antitank guns, surgical teams, bulldozers, and other supplies. At 0335, 55 Horsa gliders from the 6th British Airborne went to the east flank. For the most part, they landed pretty close to their targets. At 0354, 52 Waco gliders dropped near the west flank to reinforce the 101st Airborne, and at 0400, 46 Wacos went to the DZs for the 82nd. They faced the same challenges of enemy flak and cloud cover that the paratroopers had, causing gliders to scatter far and wide of their designated landing zones. To make matters worse, Allied intelligence had indicated the American gliders would face only short hedgerows around their LZs, but instead 40-foot trees snagged their wings and forced them to overshoot their landings. Despite just about every glider hitting something on its way down to a crash-landing outside its LZ, there were surprisingly few casualties. But once on the ground, 6-foot hedgerows made movement through the fields nearly impossible, as entrenched Germans used the roads between the hedgerows as foxholes from which to fire at the disoriented and disjointed glider-borne troops. ■

THE FIRST FREED FRENCH TOWN

Liberating Sainte-Mère-Église

The small town of Sainte-Mère-Église stands in the middle of the road between Utah and Omaha Beaches. It's easy to see why it was a key tactical location on D-Day. The 505th PIR was tasked with capturing it, but the 506th PIR arrived first—quite by accident. The 506th was supposed to land southwest of the town, but its drop was scattered, and some of the paratroopers came down within the town itself at 0115. To make a bad situation worse, a tracer set a barn on the south side of the church square on fire, and the whole town, along with the German garrison stationed there, came out to deal with the blaze. Seeing the paratroopers descend, the Germans fired, and four Allied paratroopers were killed.

When the 505th PIR dropped near the town at 0145, the Germans were on full alert. The paratroopers made easy targets, illuminated by the fire raging in the town below. Some became caught in trees, and German soldiers shot them as they hung. Private John Steele's chute snagged on the church steeple, and he hung there for hours, pretending to be dead. Despite the barn fire and the presence of Allied paratroopers, surprisingly, the town went back to sleep.

At 0400, Lieutenant Colonel Ed Krause of the 3rd Battalion of the 505th PIR led a force of about 180 men into the town. Their mission was to take Sainte-Mère-Église, and they did so easily, making it the first French town liberated in the Normandy invasion. Keeping the town, however, would be a bloody fight. Lieutenant Turner Turnbull's platoon of the 2nd Battalion of the 505th held its position north of the town through eight hours of battle, and though only 16 of the 44 men in the platoon remained effective, they held the line. Krause's 3rd guarded the south side of the town, where two German companies mounted one of the largest counterattacks on D-Day. The 3rd repulsed them, though barely, and braced while they waited for infantry to come in from the beaches.

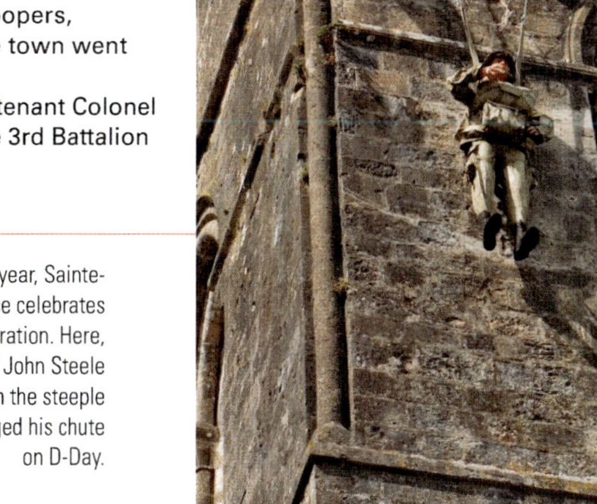

Every year, Sainte-Mère-Église celebrates its liberation. Here, a model of John Steele hangs from the steeple that snagged his chute on D-Day.

BOMBARDMENT

The Allies rained down fire and steel on German defenses, attempting to take out as many enemy positions as they could before the troops went in.

As the ships of the naval fleet approached their positions along the coast and the C-47s dropped their paratroopers and loosed their gliders inland, bombers began to take off from England. They dropped a staggering tonnage of bombs on the beach defenses, then turned back for England to refuel as the Navy continued the bombardment at first light. It was a spectacle perhaps greater than any other ever known on Earth. The Allies threw everything they had at the Germans in their very best attempt to get a foothold in continental Europe. Despite the truly awe-inspiring sight, however, the bombardment fell far short of its objectives.

Leading up to D-Day, bombers assaulted the batteries at Pas-de-Calais to keep up the Nazis' expectation that the invasion would land there. But on June 6, the main assault began. Over 1,000 Royal Air Force heavy bombers took off early in the morning, and they dropped over 5,000 tons of bombs on the German coastal defenses at the eastern invasion beaches.

At 0240, the Eighth US Air Force bombers began taking off, and they continued to take flight until 0530. Nearly 1,400 Allied aircraft bombed the Normandy coast and the city of Caen. The Allies had decimated the Luftwaffe over the first half of the year, and the German air force

A B-26, its invasion stripes blazing, flew over Sword Beach on its way back to England on D-Day. Smoke from the bombardment billowed on and behind the beach.

A dozen B-17s flew by this patrol boat on D-Day. The boat's .50-caliber machine guns are visible in the foreground.

offered little in the way of an aerial defense on D-Day.

The B-24 Liberator heavy bombers of the Eighth Air Force reached Omaha at 0555 and began their bombardment. Nearly 500 bombers dropped 1,285 tons of 100-pound bombs, but the conditions were far from ideal. As the bombers swept the narrow beaches, they were painfully aware of the Allied forces in the water just below, anywhere from 400 yards to 1 mile from shore. The bombardiers had only about 30 minutes to release their payloads, and they had to use the utmost caution not to hit their own men. They dropped 13,000 bombs from high altitudes of 15,000 to 20,000 feet, which put them out of the range of most enemy fire but also over the thick cloud cover. This meant they had to attempt to hit their targets by radar alone, which was woefully inaccurate, while not hitting their own men. As an added precaution against friendly-fire casualties, the bombardiers were ordered to wait an extra 30 seconds after they located their targets and would normally release their bombs to actually do so. Between the small targets, limited timeframe, fear of hitting Allied troops, and cloud cover, the bombing run had little effect on the German defenses. Not only did the bombers' caution cause them to drop their bombs too far inland, but over 100 of them returned home with full bays.

B-26 Marauders of the Ninth Air Force meanwhile made their way to Utah Beach. These medium bombers were designed to work with ground forces and so were well suited for the Utah area, where a significant number of Allied paratroopers were already on the ground. They flew in lower than their big B-24 brothers, dropping their 250-pound bombs at 4,000 to 6,000 feet. Sixteen of them carried 2,000-pound bombs meant to destroy heavily fortified defenses. The Marauders faced an inverse situation compared to the B-24s at Omaha: they flew under the cloud cover, which gave them clear views of their targets but also subjected them to flak and gunfire. Sergeant Ray Sanders, who was on a B-26, said, "We were accustomed to heavy flak, but this was the most withering, heavy, and accurate we ever experienced." Even so, their accuracy was unprecedented. They

B-24 Liberators fresh off the assembly line at Ford Motor Company's Willow Run plant in Michigan. They went through many test runs before being accepted by the US Army even though they had a reputation for excellence.

	B-24J LIBERATOR	B-26G MARAUDER
Wingspan	110 feet	71 feet
Length	67 feet 2 inches	58 feet 3 inches
Height	18 feet	21 feet 6 inches
Max speed	290 miles per hour	282 miles per hour
Range	1,700 miles	1,150 miles
Engines	four 1,200-horsepower Pratt & Whitney R-1830-65s	two 2,000-horsepower Pratt & Whitney R-2800-43s
Armament	ten .50-caliber machine guns, 2,700- to 8,000-pound bomb load, ball and tail turrets	twelve .50-caliber machine guns, 4,000-pound bomb load, 22-inch Mark XIII torpedo

dropped over 1 million pounds of explosives; 16 percent were direct hits, and 59 percent came within 500 feet of their targets.

THE NAVAL BOMBARDMENT

As dawn broke under the thundering bombers, the Navy began its bombardment. The first wave of infantry was already aboard the landing craft and moving in, which gave the troops a close-up view of the fire raining down on the coast. General Omar Bradley had told the 29th Infantry Division that "you men should consider yourselves lucky and are to be congratulated. You have ring-side seats at the greatest show on Earth," and what a show it was. The thundering firepower bolstered the Allied infantry's confidence and demoralized the German troops, who were being rattled around in their pillboxes.

The armada was divided into the Western Task Force for Utah and Omaha Beaches and the Eastern Task Force for Gold, Juno, and Sword. The French light cruiser *Montcalm* may have fired the first shot at 0530, or maybe it was the British light cruiser HMS *Belfast*. It could also have been the heavy cruiser USS *Quincy* or the destroyer USS *Fitch*. Regardless of which ship fired first, the bombardment began 20 minutes

The battleship USS *Nevada* fired at targets on Utah Beach using her 14-inch, 45-caliber guns.

The Unlucky Destroyers

The plane sent to drop a smoke cover for the USS *Corry* was shot down, which left the destroyer as the one ship the Germans could see. They fired on it mercilessly as it tried to take evasive action. The ship veered out of its narrow lane cleared by the minesweepers and hit a mine at 0633. Within an hour it sank, with 24 dead and 60 injured from its 276-man crew. It was one of only two destroyers that sank that day. E-boat torpedoes that missed the battleships *Ramillies* and *Warspite* sank the other, Norway's *Svenner*, which was the only Allied ship sunk by the German Navy on D-Day.

before the designated start time. Over 200 ships poured fire onto the beaches, first targeting the defenses nearest shore and then, as the minutes ticked by, moving their fire farther back to avoid hitting their own men who were moving toward shore.

At Utah, planes laid down a smoke screen to hide the Allied navy from view, allowing the warships to move in closer for the bombardment. The battleship USS *Nevada*, four cruisers, and eight destroyers led the bombardment of Utah from behind their smoke cover, but mines wreaked havoc, sinking Allied patrol boats, control craft, and landing craft along with their crews and DD tanks.

Troops boarded their LCI from an LCVP as they prepared to go ashore after the bombardment. While loading between these two craft was relatively simple, the operation was considerably more difficult when men had to climb down nets from larger ships to smaller craft.

The two battleships bombarding Omaha, the USS *Texas* and *Arkansas*, had to drop anchor because the lane that had been cleared of mines for them was so narrow, making the underwater explosives a greater threat than the coastal batteries. The warships were staggered so they could fire at their targets without crossing one another's lines of fire as they blasted the batteries. LCT(R)s—landing craft, tank (rocket)—launched 1,000 rockets. Medic W. N. Solkin, who was on one such LCT(R), said, "The ship seemed to explode. We listed sharply, and I remember being buried under arms and legs. . . . Small fires broke out and smoke rose up through the bulkheads. The heat and noise were terrific. Everyone was cursing and screaming and fighting the flames." The Western Task Force rained down hellfire until 0625, five minutes before H-Hour, which was when the men would be hitting the beaches. The Eastern Task Force kept shelling for another hour, until just before the H-Hour there.

In total, Allied planes dropped approximately 11,000 tons of bombs during the early-morning bombardment. The hundreds of guns used in the naval bombardment could fire a combined 2,000 shells in 10 minutes. The men on the landing craft who had watched shells and rockets scream over their heads and set fire to the beach just as they were making their way to shore didn't think anyone could be left alive. But despite the absolutely staggering firepower and the direct and close hits made, the batteries and pillboxes remained largely operational. The concrete strongpoints were reinforced by rebar, and though the Axis soldiers inside them were shaken and deaf, they were still able to man their guns. ■

ORDER OF THE DAY

Eisenhower on the Invasion

Every man who participated in D-Day received a copy of Eisenhower's Order of the Day, shown here. Though Eisenhower would accept "nothing less than victory," he had his doubts about whether Operation Overlord could succeed. On June 5, he would write his "in case of failure" message: "Our landings in the Cherbourg-Havre area have failed to gain a satisfactory foothold and I have withdrawn the troops. My decision to attack at this time and place was based upon the best information available. The troops, the air and the navy did all that bravery and devotion to duty could do. If any blame or fault attaches to the attempt, it is mine alone." Thankfully, he never had to deliver it.

SUPREME HEADQUARTERS
ALLIED EXPEDITIONARY FORCE

Soldiers, Sailors and Airmen of the Allied Expeditionary Force!

You are about to embark upon the Great Crusade, toward which we have striven these many months. The eyes of the world are upon you. The hopes and prayers of liberty-loving people everywhere march with you. In company with our brave Allies and brothers-in-arms on other Fronts, you will bring about the destruction of the German war machine, the elimination of Nazi tyranny over the oppressed peoples of Europe, and security for ourselves in a free world.

Your task will not be an easy one. Your enemy is well trained, well equipped and battle-hardened. He will fight savagely.

But this is the year 1944 ! Much has happened since the Nazi triumphs of 1940-41. The United Nations have inflicted upon the Germans great defeats, in open battle, man-to-man. Our air offensive has seriously reduced their strength in the air and their capacity to wage war on the ground. Our Home Fronts have given us an overwhelming superiority in weapons and munitions of war, and placed at our disposal great reserves of trained fighting men. The tide has turned ! The free men of the world are marching together to Victory !

I have full confidence in your courage, devotion to duty and skill in battle. We will accept nothing less than full Victory !

Good Luck ! And let us all beseech the blessing of Almighty God upon this great and noble undertaking.

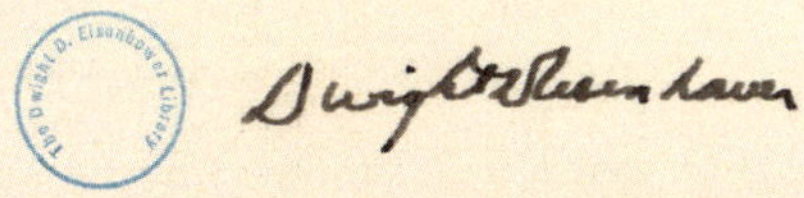

UTAH BEACH—BETTER THAN PLANNED

The Allies' meticulously laid plans fell apart before the first boots even hit the sand, which turned out to be their lucky break.

The apocalyptic thunder of the bombardment stopped for the Western Task Force. H-Hour, 0630, had arrived. The first wave of troops from the VII Corps of the First US Army stormed the 3-mile landing area code-named Utah. This beach on the eastern crook of the Cotentin Peninsula hooked diagonally north instead of running pretty much straight east–west like the other invasion beaches. The plan involved three sectors: Tare Green to the northeast, Uncle Red in the middle, and Victor on the southwest end. The four causeways exiting the beach led right into the fields that Rommel had flooded to bolster the meager fixed defenses in the area. So, while the beach was not heavily defended, the narrow roads through the sunken lowlands behind it were obstacles no other beach had.

Twenty Higgins boats—each carrying 30 troops of the 2nd Battalion of the 8th Infantry Regiment, 4th Division—followed in the wake of 32 DD tanks.

A weapons carrier drove through the surf to land on Utah Beach. The gunner aimed skyward in case of an air attack.

Carefully timed waves of assault teams, combat engineers, vehicles, and artillery were supposed to follow, but the plan went to hell right from the start. Mines had claimed almost all of the LCC boats assigned to direct traffic. Only one of the four sent out remained operational, making for chaos on the water. LCTs and other landing craft scrambled to figure out where they were supposed to be. Strong tides and heavy winds pushed and pulled the boats off course, and thick smoke blinded the coxswains.

Landing craft crashed into mines in the chaos until Lieutenant Howard Vander Beek of LLC 60 took command of the situation. Vander Beek led LCTs and Higgins boats toward the beach, directing the LCTs to drop ramp at 3,000 yards instead of 5,000 to cut down on time. The tanks were supposed to land first, but the Higgins boats passed them. Sergeant Malvin Pike of Company E, the first company to land, reported, "I jumped out in waist-deep water. We had 200 feet to go to shore and you couldn't run, you could just kind of push forward.

Columns of men waded ashore from their landing craft at Utah Beach. Barrage balloons mixed with the storm clouds.

Strongpoints

The invasion beaches had two types of resistance strongpoints: *Widerstandsnester*, meaning "resistance nests," which were reinforced positions, and *Stützpunkte*, which were larger support positions. The strongpoints had a vast range of armament, but typically had a few bunkers housing a platoon of about 40, reinforced concrete pits (called *Tobruks*) for smaller guns, and some larger artillery guns. Small strongpoints dotted the causeways at Utah, but the major Stützpunkt was at Les Dunes de Varreville at the north end. It had two 8.8-centimeter artillery guns, five Tobruks for 37-millimeter guns, and four machine-gun nests.

The landing plan fell apart, to the troops' good fortune. The planned landing zones are to the right on this map, while the actual landing spots are indicated on the left.

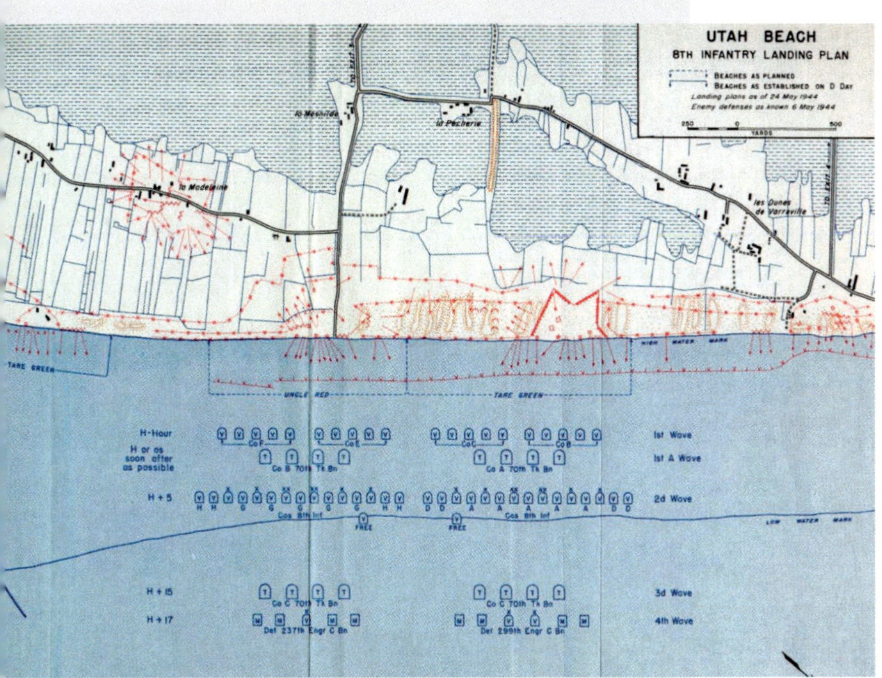

We finally made it to the edge of the water, then we had 200 yards of open beach to cross, through obstacles. But fortunately most of the Germans were not able to fight, they were all shook up from the bombing and the shelling and the rockets and most of them just wanted to surrender."

They were 2,000 yards south of their targets, landing around Exit 2 instead of spread out from there to the strongpoint of Les Dunes de Varreville in the north. The chaos from the water could have carried over to the beach had it not been for Brigadier General Theodore Roosevelt Jr., son of the former president. He was on the first boat to land and immediately took command of the situation. As

Belgian gates (top) and hedgehogs (bottom) were common obstacles used by the Germans to fortify the Atlantic Wall. On their own, they could prevent craft and tank movement, but explosives were often affixed to them, which made them deadly.

luck would have it, the spot where they had landed wasn't as heavily fortified as the target landing zones to the north. Instead of facing two strongpoints, they faced only one, which had been pounded by B-26 attacks; the German troops inside had yet to rally. Roosevelt made a reconnaissance of the rear of the beach and found the causeway exits. He reported their position to Colonel James Van Fleet, the commanding officer of the 8th Infantry Regiment, who had just waded to shore. Van Fleet had actually wanted to land in this area originally, but the Navy had fought him on it. Roosevelt and Van Fleet faced a big decision: fight here or make their way to the intended landing areas. Roosevelt reportedly made the famous remark, "We'll start the war from right here." And they did.

IN COME THE ENGINEERS

The landing went incredibly well given the chaos and confusion at the start, but the Allied forces needed to clear the beaches of their deadly obstacles that Rommel had planted to fortify his Atlantic Wall. Steel obstacles included spikes, crossbeam structures called "hedgehogs," and Belgian gates. The spikes and hedgehogs usually were fixed between the high and low tide marks, where they would be hidden or visible depending on the tide. Alone, they punctured hulls and destroyed landing craft, but the Germans sometimes attached explosives to them, making them even deadlier. The Nazis also scattered Belgian gates on the beaches to disrupt vehicles and block exits. Tank dozers could run down these obstacles, but more often engineers and demo teams destroyed them with hand charges.

The Naval demolition teams of the 2nd Naval Beach Battalion and Army Engineer teams of the 1st Engineer Special Brigade had the job of destroying these obstacles. The teams were supposed to come ashore at H+5 and H+15, respectively, but they beached pretty much together in the second wave. This deviation from the plan turned out to be another fortuitous mishap. By this time, the German troops were over the shock of the bombardment and firing across the beach. Since the demo teams and

Troops made their way across Utah Beach and then rested in the shelter of the seawall. Here, soldiers moved out over the wall to take inland objectives behind the beach.

engineers worked simultaneously, they swiftly cleared the obstacles, allowing the men and vehicles to quickly make their way up the beach once the shooting began.

The demolition teams blew the obstacles the rising tide would have otherwise covered, while the engineers cleared obstacles above the tide line using hand charges, tanks, and tank dozers. In less than an hour, they'd cleared eight gaps 50 yards wide or more. With the obstacles cleared, the engineers blew holes in the seawall and took out the barbed wire that lined its front and back. Then they cleared paths through the mines in the dunes behind the wall and joined the assaults the infantry was conducting against the fortifications.

Medics, reconnaissance troops, MPs, and counterintelligence corpsmen also came in with this second wave. Lieutenant Elliot Richardson, commanding officer of a medic detachment, recalled, "I walked up to the top of the dune and looked around. There was this barbed wire area and a wounded officer who had stepped on an anti-personnel mine calling for help. . . . I walked in toward him, putting each foot down, carefully and picked him up and carried him back. . . . That was my baptism." The author J. D. Salinger was there with the 4th Counter Intelligence Corps. He reportedly carried drafts of chapters from *Catcher in the Rye* with him.

MORE MEN, MORE SUCCESS

The third wave beached at H+15: eight more LCTs from the 70th Tank Battalion carrying M4 and dozer tanks. The fourth wave had

"THERE WAS THIS BARBED WIRE AREA AND A WOUNDED OFFICER WHO HAD STEPPED ON AN ANTIPERSONNEL MINE CALLING FOR HELP."

—LIEUTENANT ELLIOT RICHARDSON

One soldier looked into the camera as his group disembarked their landing craft and made their way through the breakers and onto Utah Beach.

German prisoners were kept in a barbed-wire pen at Utah Beach. Behind them a group of African-American soldiers looked on.

members of the 237th and 299th Engineer Combat Battalions, as well as two more battalions from the 8th and 22nd Regiments. First elements of the 90th Infantry Division came ashore, but the remainder wouldn't join the action until June 10. The waves of men faced whoever remained from the elements of the 91st, 243rd, and 709th German infantry divisions stationed in the area. Some German soldiers were still in their strongpoints, but the bombardment had driven many of them from their fortifications and into trenches behind the dunes. The Allies captured who they could and sent them to the USS *Bayfield.* Those they couldn't capture, they killed. By 0900, US troops had secured three of the four exits and were heading inland. They suffered just 197 casualties, including 60 missing. By the end of the day, 23,250 troops were ashore. ■

MEDAL OF HONOR

Theodore Roosevelt Jr.

Theodore "Ted" Roosevelt Jr. was no stranger to war when he waded up to Utah Beach on D-Day. In World War I, he had commanded the 26th Infantry Regiment and fearlessly led his men into battle, even in the face of enemy fire and mustard gas. In his zeal to capture a machine gun during the Battle of Soissons (France, 1918), he charged into action but forgot his helmet. Fortunately, although he was shot, it was through the knee instead of the head.

When America entered World War II, Ted was in his mid-50s—an accomplished politician, businessman, and founding member of the American Legion. Despite a heart condition and a bad leg that made him walk with a cane, he wanted to fight. He rose to the rank of brigadier general as he made his way through Algeria, Sicily, and Sardinia. In 1944, the army sent him to England to help plan the invasion. While there, he suffered a serious bout of pneumonia, but he still wanted to be with his men of the 4th Division, storming Utah in the first wave. The division's commander Major General Raymond "Tubby" Barton didn't like this idea, fearing Ted wasn't strong enough, but Ted was relentless. He was also a phenomenal leader, and Barton reluctantly granted his request to go ashore just a week before the invasion.

Brigadier General Ted Roosevelt Jr. during the Allied invasion of Sicily, 1943.

Brigadier General Roosevelt was in the first boat ashore, and when he realized the boats were coming in south of their objective, he personally made a reconnaissance of the rear of the beach. He conferred with other commanders, and they decided to attack the enemy positions where they stood instead of hiking across exposed beach to their target. Ted led this impromptu plan, which worked beautifully with little confusion. He strode up and down the beach, directing traffic, greeting soldiers as they landed, and directing them beyond the seawall. His hand was hit by shrapnel, but he kept on joking with his men, keeping their spirits up and leading them as few other men could. Utah was a success, and Ted played a large part in that.

Just over a month later, he died of heart of attack while still in Normandy. On September 28, he was posthumously awarded the Medal of Honor for his actions at D-Day:

> *"He repeatedly led groups from the beach, over the seawall, and established them inland. His valor, courage, and presence in the very front of the attack and his complete unconcern at being under heavy fire inspired the troops to heights of enthusiasm and self-sacrifice. Although the enemy had the beach under constant direct fire, Brig. Gen. Roosevelt moved from one locality to another, rallying men around him, directed and personally led them against the enemy. He thus contributed substantially to the successful establishment of the beachhead in France."*

Years later, General Omar Bradley, commander of the US zones, wrote, "I have never known a braver man, nor a more devoted soldier."

BLOODY OMAHA

As H-Hour struck, everything went wrong at Omaha Beach. Within minutes, the Allies knew they were watching a tragedy unfold.

As well as things went at Utah, they went tragically wrong at Omaha in practically equal measure. While Ted Roosevelt joked with his men just one beach over, his son Quentin struggled to get onto Omaha Beach in the first wave of troops. The bombardment had been largely ineffective at Omaha, and enemy fire was heavier than anticipated. Things didn't go according to plan on either beach, but all the luck seemed to be at Utah. Every inch of Omaha was a bloody struggle, as 34,200 troops from the experienced 1st and relatively green 29 Infantry Divisions, V Corps of the First US Army, pushed through the deadly gauntlet of Rommel's formidable fortifications.

The area code-named Omaha stretched out over a 5-mile crescent, from a small fishing village in the east to the mouth of the Vire river to the west. The beach itself was a bank of shingle—stones ranging from the size of pebbles to cobbles, which were difficult for tanks to traverse. The shingle bank sloped upward for anywhere from 3 to 50 feet to meet a 10-foot seawall in the west and sand dunes in the east. Behind the wall there were a paved promenade and

Men battled their way through surf and enemy fire from their LCVPs to reach the beach code-named Omaha, which saw the fiercest fighting on all of D-Day.

A Sherman tank fitted for amphibious use mired on an invasion beach. Though it had already shed its inflatable skirt, the raised air intakes on its back show that it was an amphibious tank.

an antitank ditch. Behind the dunes was a sand shelf up to 220 yards wide. Both the wall and dunes were backed by 100-foot-high bluffs, meaning the five exits off the beach were vitally important.

Rommel took advantage of this narrow, curved stretch of beach by aiming most of his guns not into the water but across the beach. As the Allies struggled ashore, the Germans caught them in a vicious network of crossfire. Thirteen Widerstandsnester with pillboxes, Tobruks, machine-gun nests, heavy artillery, and shallow trenches for small-arms fire were connected by deep trenches and tunnels. This imposing line of fortifications protected the beach exits and crowned the bluffs. Mines studded the water, promenade, and bluffs. Barbed and concertina wire lined everything. Artillery batteries 6 miles inland could shell the beach, creating shrapnel blasts 60 feet wide. The troops would have to swim ashore under fire from every angle.

The Allies counted on two things when they planned their face-off with the Germans on Omaha Beach. First, their 34,200 men would be up against the 716th Division, an Ost battalion. Half of those 800 or so men were Polish and Russian troops who didn't want to be there in the first place. Second, the bombardment would take out a lot of the defenses while making craters on the beach. The troops could then use those craters as foxholes to protect themselves from the crossfire.

The planners were wrong on both counts. The bombardment at Omaha was largely ineffective; the bombers dropped their loads too far inland, and the naval bombardment was inaccurate and unproductive. The Allies' intelligence on the German forces in the area was also woefully inaccurate; they had no idea the German High Command had moved part of the capable, veteran 352nd Infantry Division to the area. The US troops at Omaha would in fact face three battalions of Axis troops at the beach, not one.

0625 The landing craft of the first wave were dragged out of position by winds of up to 18 knots that kicked up 3- to 4-foot waves. A typical LCVP (landing craft vehicle & personnel) carried 31 to 36 men and one officer. Some crews consisting of five riflemen carrying 96 rounds of ammunition for their M1s were the first men out of the boat. Four men armed with rifles and wire cutters and two more men with larger "search-nose" cutters followed. Two assault-rifle teams of two men each carrying nine hundred rounds for each gun were next. They were followed by four men who composed two bazooka teams, a mortar team of four men, two men on a flamethrower crew, and finally five demolition men.

In the boats, the men were cold, drenched, and seasick. But they had trained for this. The waves swamped almost a dozen boats, and DD tanks, which were supposed to land first, sank with their crews inside. One group of LCTs in the first wave only managed to get two of their 29 tanks ashore. The next launch went right up to the beach; half of the tanks made it from this group.

0630 H-Hour. The naval guns moved their fire to inland targets, while fighter planes continued to cover the beach. Two battalions from the 116th Regiment of the 29th Division had set out for the four western sectors: Dog Green, Dog White, Dog Red, and Easy Green. Two battalions from the 16th Regiment of the 1st Division—known as the "Big Red One" and the only veteran force at Omaha—were supposed to beach at Easy Red and Fox Green. Landing craft grounded on sandbars 50 to 100 yards out. Men got off the boats in 3- and 4-foot breakers. Only Company A of the 116th came ashore on target. The other companies beached anywhere from a few yards to over a mile east of their targets. Intense fire strafed men on the landing-craft ramps and followed them as they struggled through rough water that reached their chests. Their heavy packs, up to 100 pounds, pulled at them, and some drowned under the weight. Men died en masse before they even made it to the beach. In the first minutes of D-Day, Omaha was already a tragedy.

0635 As the men tried to come ashore, they realized the bombardment had not destroyed the fixed fortifications as promised, nor had it created foxholes in which they could take cover. Companies intermingled, and the men were confused, unable to find their commanding officers. They were exhausted and seasick and still had to cross up to 200 yards of open beach before they could get under the cover of the seawall or shingle bank. They sheltered behind obstacles before moving on, which prevented the engineers from doing their jobs. Success depended on small assault units achieving specific tasks in specific places—taking out defenses, clearing obstacles in the intertidal zone before the sea could cover them, providing covering fire—but for most of the men in the first wave, just surviving unscathed seemed impossible. In fact, they only had a one in two chance of making it.

At Dog Green, Company A of the 116th and C of the 2nd Rangers came in on their targets, only to

German guns hit men before they were even off their landing craft. Here, troops crouched inside an LCVP as they approached Omaha Beach to avoid the enemy fire.

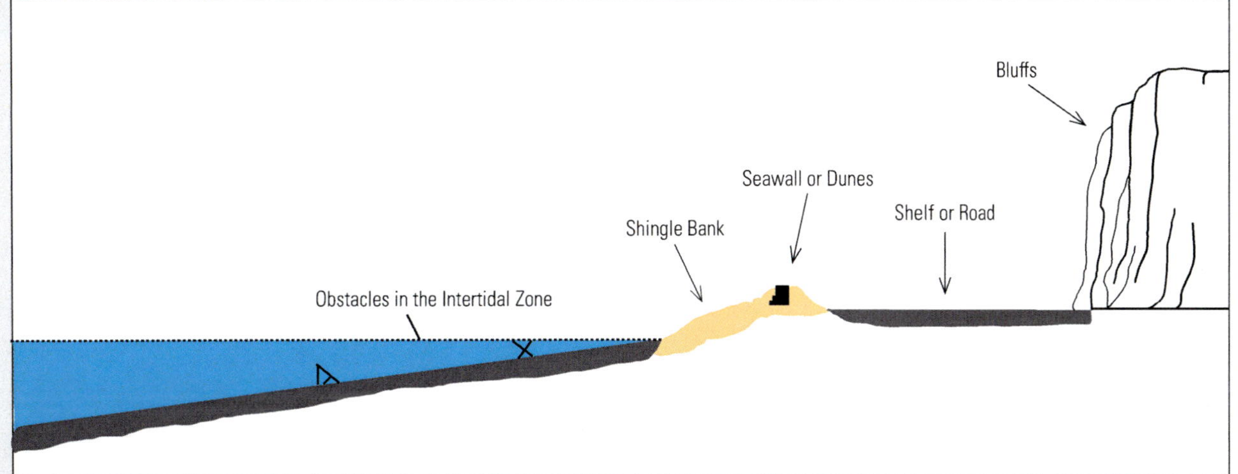

In addition to the German defenses, the terrain at Omaha Beach posed significant challenges for the soldiers attempting to cross it and make their way inland.

Troops as they landed on Omaha Beach. The LCI where this photograph was taken was shelled and left a wreck on the beach later in the day.

meet some of the most intense and accurate counterfire of the day, which came from the defenses at exit D-1. Mortar fire practically disintegrated landing craft. There was virtually no shelter, and men tried to take cover in the water itself. Beachmaster Lieutenant Joe Smith watched boats get vaporized. He recalled that on one landing craft, "A German machine gun or two opened up and you could see the sand kick up right in front of the boat. No one moved. The coxswain stood up and yelled . . . 'For Christ's sake, fellas, get out! I've got to go get another load!'"

Soldiers formed a firing line even though they had not an inch of cover. Nearly every one of them was a casualty. As the tide came in, the injured drowned. Company A suffered up to two-thirds casualties. The rangers lost 35 of their 64-man company.

Companies E and F of the 16th were supposed to assault the mile-long stretch of Easy Red, but the water pushed both east. Lost members of the 116th and other 16th companies were the only infantry in the first wave to come ashore at Easy Red. They came down the ramps of the landing craft into water up to their necks and had to drop some of their best weapons and supplies just to get to shore. While much of the 116th made it to the shingle bank with relative ease, the 16th had suffered almost 50 percent casualties.

0640 Some of Company G of the 116th landed on Dog Red instead of its target, Dog White. The grass on the bluff was on fire, and the smoke gave the men cover as they crossed the beach. Relatively unscathed, they took cover behind the shingle bank. Other sections of Company G, however, were pushed farther east to Easy Green, where they took heavier fire and suffered high rates of casualties.

Company F landed near its target in front of exit D-3, a heavily fortified point. It took three of the sections 45 minutes to cross the beach, during which time they suffered 50 percent casualties. The remaining sections lost their officers, and when the men made it to the shingle bank, they were in chaos.

"A GERMAN MACHINE GUN OR TWO OPENED UP AND YOU COULD SEE THE SAND KICK UP RIGHT IN FRONT OF THE BOAT."

—BEACHMASTER LIEUTENANT JOE SMITH

Medics gave a plasma transfusion to an injured soldier on Fox Green. His landing craft was sunk off shore, and his inflatable life belt was then used as a pillow.

The majority of the first wave of the 16th came ashore east of their targets, landing at Fox Green. Company F as well as Companies E from both the 16th and 116th were badly scattered along this beach. The Germans fired on them as soon as their ramps came down, and they suffered heavy casualties. In one case, just seven men made it from their boat to the shingle bank.

0655 Naval Combat Demolition Units as well as the 146th and 299th Army Engineer Battalions were scheduled to land at H+03, H+08, and H+25. Their job was to clear obstacles from 16 50-yard breaches, mark the cleared lanes, and get off

Famous People at Omaha

Before he was a baseball legend, Yogi Berra was a Seaman 1st class assigned to an LCSS, a 36-foot flat-bottomed boat with a rocket launcher that provided cover for troops on Omaha. Although there were no casualties on his boat, one man was killed after getting off and going ashore.

Author Ernest Hemingway, who was a war correspondent for *Collier's* on D-Day, rode an LCVP up to Omaha with the seventh wave. He later reported that "it had been a frontal assault in broad daylight, against a mined beach defended by all the obstacles military ingenuity could devise." Martha Gellhorn, a fellow war correspondent and Hemingway's wife, did not receive official permission to go in with the invasion, but she stowed away in a bathroom on a hospital ship and went ashore with an ambulance team.

John Ford, the director of many classic Westerns, was the head of the photographic unit charged with recording D-Day. He has given a vivid account of going ashore, but his biographers doubt that his story is true.

Coast Guard troops watched a mine explode right in front of them as they nosed their LCI toward shore. The coxswains and gun crews piloting the landing craft faced hidden obstacles as well as enemy fire over and over as they brought troops to the shoreline.

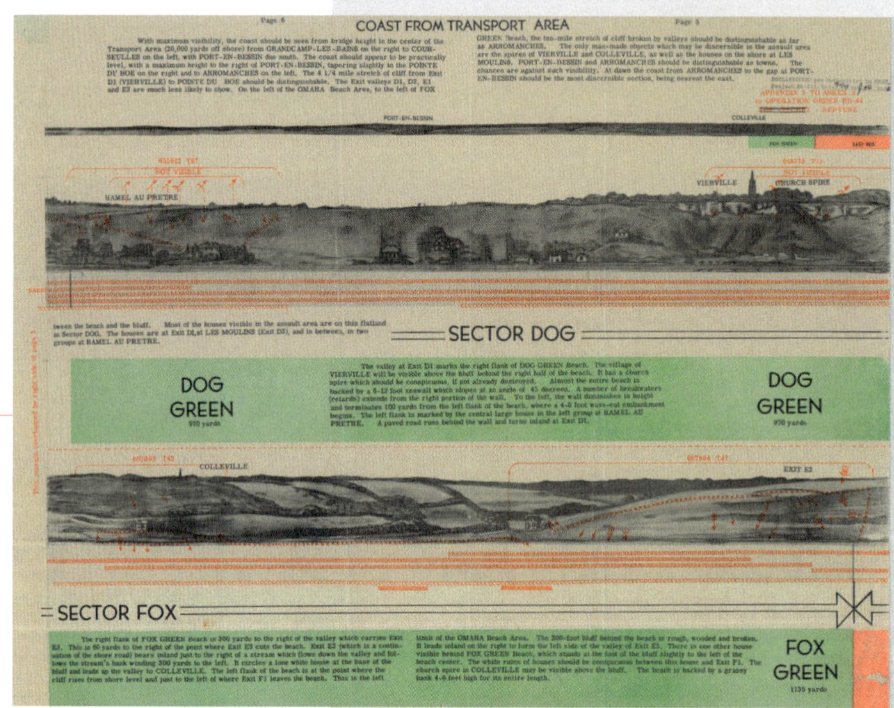

Sector charts of Omaha Beach gave troops in-depth descriptions and sketches of the invasion area so they would be able to orient themselves using landmarks.

the beach by H+30. At H+25, 0655, teams were still just trying to get onto the beach. When they did land, they were off target. Troops and tank groups were supposed to give them cover, but many of the tanks had sunk, and fire had largely pinned down the infantry. Sergeant William Garland of the 146th Army Engineer Battalion recalled, "The men thought the infantry would be ahead of them, but the beach was innocent of footprints."

When they did land near infantrymen, those soldiers often got in their way, taking cover behind obstacles set to blow or sheltering behind the few dozers that had made it to the beach. Even with all of these challenges, the engineer and demo teams made it a long way toward achieving their objectives. By the time the tide was too high for them to work, against all odds, they'd cleared six complete breaches and three partial ones, mostly on the eastern side of the beach. But the cost was steep, at roughly 41 percent casualties, most of them suffered during the first 30 minutes.

0700 Company L of the 16th came in 30 minutes late and on the

This map shows the obstacles that fortified the shingle in front of the exits off Omaha that led to the town of Colleville-sur-Mer. It is stamped "TOP SECRET—BIGOT" meaning it was classified as "British Invasion of German Occupied Territory": the highest level of security.

opposite end of Fox Green from the place they had planned to land. Some groups that came in at the edge of the beach, where the bluffs started to rise, didn't suffer any casualties. They assaulted the bluffs—the only company in the first wave able to operate after crossing the beach.

Across the rest of Omaha, the men who'd made it onto the beach took cover behind whatever they could find as the second wave started to arrive.

0710 More companies landed in the confusion.

0715 Ranger battalions that were supposed to capture Pointe du Hoc diverted to the Dog sectors to assist in the assault on Omaha. Companies A and B of the 2nd Battalion encountered the same obstacles and heavy fire at Dog Green as the infantry that had come before them, suffering about 50 percent casualties. The 5th Battalion fared far better at Dog White, where it lost only a handful of its 450 men before making it to the seawall.

0720 Yet more companies came ashore, including mortar

"THE MEN THOUGHT THE INFANTRY WOULD BE AHEAD OF THEM, BUT THE BEACH WAS INNOCENT OF FOOTPRINTS." —SERGEANT WILLIAM GARLAND

The obstacle belt, casualties, a swamped tank and trucks, and a beached LCT are all visible in this photograph, which captures many of the hardships and tragedies at Omaha.

battalions, in an even bigger assault wave than the first. The exits still weren't cleared. No one had made it off the beach, and the second wave repeated the tragedies of the first wave on an even larger scale. Tanks, jeeps, trucks, and artillery all attempted to get ashore, creating deadly congestion instead of providing cover and plowing through exits. Landing craft came in off target, their men slaughtered by relentless German fire. Those who managed to find cover were leaderless and pinned. The tide was rising over the obstacles. The crucial and carefully planned timing of the invasion was in tatters, and waves churned red on the beach.

0730 It was H+1, and the Americans hadn't yet achieved the objectives scheduled for the first minutes of the landing. Bodies, vehicles, and confused infantry choked Dog White. Still more men were coming in, including the command group of the 116th on LCVP 71. On their way to the beach, they dodged obstacles and hit a mine, which by some miracle did not explode. Once on shore, Brigadier General Norman Cota made his way to the seawall and assessed the situation. No one had breached the wall yet, and the men huddled there were pinned down by machine-gun fire. Cota realized they couldn't make it up the draws to the exits, nor could they stay where they were. They would have to go over the wall, through the minefield, and climb the bluffs.

0740 The obstacle belt was now barely visible, which held up landing craft, often carrying headquarters and medic teams, as the inland batteries poured shells down onto the beach.

The 320th Barrage Balloon Battalion (Colored)

In 1944, the US Army segregated its troops, and very few African-American troops were allowed to participate in D-Day. About 1,200 black troops landed at Utah, and they were mostly drivers. Black members of the Coast Guard drove Higgins boats, and there were some African-American sailors on the warships, but the all-black 320th Barrage Balloon Battalion (Colored) was the only one of its kind. Its soldiers brought in barrage balloons to prevent strafing from the Luftwaffe, which, except for a flyby from a couple planes, proved absent at Omaha.

Troops from the 16th Regiment, 1st Infantry Division, gathered on a narrow strip of beach where bodies awaited burial.

0745 The tide came in, making the beach, which still had no exits, even narrower. Some areas behind the shingle bank were packed to capacity. Incoming men couldn't shelter there; all they could do was lie in the open sand and pray.

All plans had gone out the window; the men just had to get off the beach. Across all the sectors, small groups realized their only hope was to climb the bluffs. Major Sidney Bingham, 2nd Battalion, 116th Division, later said, "The individual and small-unit initiative carried the day. Very little, if any, credit can be accorded company, battalion, or regimental commanders for their tactical prowess and/or their coordination of the action."

0800 The tide now covered the obstacle belt. Colonel George Taylor of the 16th Regiment, 1st Division, landed near exit E-3 on Fox Green. After making it to the seawall, he rallied groups of men around him, famously saying, "There are only two kinds of people on this beach: the dead and those about to die. So let's get the hell out of here!" He had his eye on the bluffs. "If we're going to die, let's die up there!" He used bangalore torpedoes to blow gaps in the barbed wire, his engineers marked paths through the minefields, and his men pressed through to assault pillboxes with flamethrowers and dynamite charges.

0830 Back at Dog White, Company B of the 116th, under the command of General Cota, and the 5th Ranger Battalion worked their way across 150 yards of open, flat ground. They then climbed the sloping bluff in narrow columns, trying to avoid the mines that studded the hillside. Smoke covered them as they made their careful ascent, and by 0830 the first men were on top of the bluff. As those first troops cleared Germans out of the trenches, the last men were leaving the seawall. They had made the most important penetration on the western beaches for all of D-Day.

While this first big success was underway, no one had yet been able to clear the exits, and the traffic on the beach was at a critical mass. The 7th Naval Beach Battalion halted all vehicle landings and called back craft heading to the beach, which caused its own confusion on the water. A traffic jam built up in the waves; more landing craft swamped, and more tanks sank.

Troops on an LCVP headed to shore watched their compatriots take cover behind whatever they could find as a single column of men picked their way up the smoky bluff.

0900 Commander W. J. Marshall of the USS *Satterlee* was flummoxed. "It was most galling and depressing to lie idly a few hundred yards off the beaches and watch our troops, tanks, landing boats, and motor vehicles being heavily shelled and not able to fire a shot to help them just because we had no information as to what to shoot at and were unable to detect the source of enemy fire."

Lieutenant Commander Ralph "Rebel" Ramey of the destroyer USS *McCook* was also tired of watching the events unfold. He moved his guns from his assigned targets to targets of opportunity. He sailed to the west end of Omaha, taking his ship in closer to the shore than was allowed, and blasted the fortifications around the Vierville exit. After an hour, he had destroyed two of the big German guns.

Meanwhile, the infantry's intense training was paying off. They began to rally, improvising small groups led by whoever had the courage to take charge. They used the assault tactics that their training

A US Navy destroyer, Gleaves class, bombarded the coast with its 5/38 guns. Destroyers played an integral part in providing the cover US troops needed to eventually cross Omaha Beach.

"IT WAS MOST GALLING AND DEPRESSING TO LIE IDLY A FEW HUNDRED YARDS OFF THE BEACHES."

—COMMANDER W. J. MARSHALL

Spent cartridges and powder tanks littered the deck of the USS *Hobson*, a destroyer that provided fire support on D-Day.

had drilled into them over and over. Cota's penetration area east of Dog White widened.

At Easy Green and Red, rifle companies of the 3rd Battalion, 116th, got past the bluffs. Company I cut breaches into the wire at exit D-3. The men carefully picked their way up the mined bluff for half an hour, and when they reached the top, they encountered exactly zero enemy troops.

0930 All across Omaha, troops ascended the bluffs and flanked the Germans' fortifications, capturing or killing the soldiers inside. The Ost battalion men were quick to surrender and talk. They provided valuable intelligence on where German troops were positioned, which gave the Allies at Omaha a much-needed edge.

0950 The Navy ordered all the destroyers supporting Omaha to redirect their fire to targets of opportunity. The ships came in close enough to scrape the seabed as they fired their 5-inch shells at pillboxes and even individual riflemen—they were that close. They risked running aground, but their fire helped the men on the beach make progress. Admiral C. F. Bryant ordered over the TBS radio, "Get on them, men! Get on them! They are raising hell with the men on the beach, and we can't have any more of that! We must stop it!"

1000 As men got clear of the beaches, albeit not by the intended exits, reinforcements arrived. The sectors, however, still were in chaos. At Easy Red, vehicles and tanks still clogged the beach, and the Germans on the high ground still pinned down troops with fire.

1130 A battleship 1,000 yards off shore near exit E-1 on Easy Red fired on an active pillbox, which quickly surrendered. Engineers cleared mines from the exit, and men were finally able to funnel off that section of beach. Command sent more troops that way. Subsequent landings caused further congestion, but traffic was now the problem here—not enemy fire—and once the engineers cut a road big enough for vehicles to pass over, even that cleared. The day was turning around. As yet more landing groups came in, they quickly crossed this area of the beach.

1200 The 2nd Battalion of the 18th Regiment, 1st Division, came ashore at Easy Red. Naval fire targeted the strongpoints protecting exit D-1 and took out the fortifications there within an hour. Although the fortifications were largely clear, inland artillery fire prevented troops from using the exit.

1300 The 3rd and 1st Battalions of the 18th Regiment landed at Easy Red roughly three hours late due to the congestion. The 115th Regiment landed in a group instead of in intervals, and it took them an hour to get up the beach to the exit. Although the Allies had cleared the beach defenses at exits D-1, E-1, and F-1, the Germans still held D-3 and E-3.

1400 The Navy reopened the beaches for vehicles, which poured ashore for the rest of the day.

1500 Reinforcements arrived. The 336th Battalion, which was scheduled to land at Easy Red and march on Fox Beach, landed 4,000 yards from its target and began the hard trek across the beach under

Wounded men from the 3rd Battalion, 16th Infantry Regiment, 1st Division, received medical attention and then food and cigarettes.

A German pillbox knocked out by Allied aircraft. The concrete walls of these gun emplacements were 13 feet thick and reinforced with steel, making them near impossible to destroy.

almost constant fire from inland batteries. Company G was still fighting to clear a pillbox at exit E-3 when the 2nd Battalion of the 18th arrived to relieve them. Artillery and mortar fire barraged E-3 until dark.

1700 The 336th reached F-1, having two men killed and 27 injured. Those who had made it cleared a 12-foot road, and command redirected landing traffic to take advantage of it. Meanwhile, tanks from the 741st Tank Battalion moved inland from exit E-1.

2000 The 745th Tank Battalion reached the high ground behind F-1 as darkness fell.

2400 By midnight, tanks were finally able to use exit E-3. The day was a hard-won success. Even so, D-Day at Omaha Beach saw over two thousand Allied casualties, and the morning is still remembered as a catastrophe. The exact number of men killed and injured there is unknown and will never be known. The best estimates from a history by the V Corps put the number of Allied casualties at 2,374, comprising 331 missing, 1,349 wounded, and 694 killed. The large majority of those casualties happened during the first 30 minutes of the assault. ■

A sketch of the dress and supplies for a platoon leader from the 29th Infantry Division. This drawing was made by the division's Lieutenant Jack Shea.

Hard-Won Pointe du Hoc

West of the Omaha Beach sectors stands Pointe du Hoc, a rocky promontory jutting out into the Channel. Command identified it as a key position during planning because its 100-foot-high cliff served as an elevated vantage point between Omaha and Utah, crowned by a battery of 155-millimeter guns that could fire on both beaches. Rommel had stationed his formidable 352nd Infantry at Pointe du Hoc, so while it was critically important for the Allies to capture this crag of rock, it would be incredibly difficult to do so. The planners assigned this dangerous mission to the Rangers. Lieutenant Colonel James Rudder commanded members of the 2nd Ranger Battalion, and Lieutenant Colonel Max Schneider led the 5th Ranger Battalion, which would serve as support.

The 2nd Battalion planned for Companies E and F to land on the east side of the promontory while D would come up on the west. They would come over in LCAs (landing craft, artillery) as well as four DUKWs (amphibious trucks) equipped with extension ladders from the London Fire Department, which the Rangers would use to scale the cliff. Company C, meanwhile, would land on Charlie, the westernmost beach at Omaha, and take out the guns that topped the cliffs of Pointe de la Percée. They would then move west to clear out any enemies still holding their position between la Percée and du Hoc. Companies A and B and the 5th Battalion would wait in landing craft offshore, looking to Pointe du Hoc for the signal to land. If no signal came, they were to land on Omaha and attack du Hoc from the rear. This plan, like all the plans for Utah and Omaha, went to hell.

The battleship USS *Texas* and the destroyers USS *Satterlee* and HMS *Talybont* bombarded Pointe du Hoc in the morning. The Rangers set out at H-Hour, but before they even got to the

At Pointe du Hoc, Rangers demonstrated the ladders they used to storm the cliff. While they weren't able to make use of the fire brigade ladders brought on the DUKWs, they still made it up the cliff.

Rangers rested and got aid atop Pointe du Hoc after achieving one of the most dangerous objectives set for D-Day.

cliffs, an LCA capsized, and the mission was down 22 men. As the remaining Rangers approached their targets at H-Hour, Germans poured down heavy fire. By the time Company C got to the base of Pointe de la Percée, the 70-man team was down to 35. They still managed to climb the cliff, take out the defenses at the top, and get underway to Pointe du Hoc, but by the time they moved out, only twelve men were left.

Wind and waves pushed the LCAs carrying Companies E, F, and D off course by 3 miles, all the way to la Percée. The boats did not get to du Hoc until 0710, 40 minutes later than planned. This gave the Germans 45 minutes to rally after the morning's bombardment. All three companies landed on the east side of the promontory under heavy fire. The DUKWs couldn't cross the rocky beach, so the Rangers scaled the cliffs using ladders propped up on piles of rubble and ropes that were waterlogged and slippery. Their intense training paid dividends, and they surmounted the cliff in minutes despite the bullets and grenades that rained down on them.

Once on top, the Rangers set up Browning Automatic Rifles and cleared out the German soldiers. They looked around at the destruction from the morning's bombardment and the air strikes waged over the previous month. The fearsome guns were gone.

The Rangers cut off the road behind Pointe du Hoc and moved to clear the surrounding area. It didn't take them long to discover that the Germans had repositioned the guns, which were now trained on Utah. The Rangers used thermite grenades to melt the breeches of the guns, rendering them useless.

Schneider and his 5th Battalion offshore never saw a signal come from Pointe du Hoc, so at 0715, they landed near Vierville and exit D-1 with the intention of taking Pointe du Hoc from the rear as planned. This was a fortunate turn of events for Major Cote and the 29th Infantry, who were struggling to get clear of the area. The Rangers joined them, and they made critical progress inland. Together, they established a beachhead, where they were joined by more infantrymen and paratroopers.

The separated Ranger companies from the 2nd Battalion who were holding the road behind Pointe du Hoc tried to regroup. The Germans began a series of counterattacks at 2300, which didn't stop until 0300 on June 7. The Rangers were desperate for reinforcements, but the intense fighting and casualties all across Omaha meant that they were slow to arrive just about everywhere. When a battalion from the 116th finally arrived on the morning of the 8th to relieve them, fewer than 75 of the 225 Rudder's Rangers were still fit for duty. Of the 2nd Battalion on the whole, 77 were dead, 152 were wounded, and 38 were missing. From the 5th, 23 were dead, 89 were wounded, and two were missing. These 381 casualties compose 16 percent of the total casualties at Omaha—a substantial portion of the cost in the incredibly steep price of victory at Omaha.

H-HOUR FOR THE OTHER ALLIES

British and Canadian troops pushed across the beaches along the east side of the Calvados coast, facing deadly enemy fire.

After an hour of fighting at Utah and Omaha, H-Hour came up for the British Second Army and the eastern invasion beaches. All across the Calvados coast, the dunes smoked and guns roared as landing craft packed with British and Canadian troops fought their way through the waves to their targets. At Gold, the westernmost beach of the Eastern Task Force, troops needed to capture the port town of Arromanches, establish a beachhead, cut off the Caen–Bayeux highway behind the beach, and link Omaha to Juno. Juno Beach was east of Gold, dotted with small fishing villages and bordered by fortified dunes. Carpiquet airfield was inland from Juno, and capturing that was one of the biggest objectives for the day. The troops storming Sword Beach at the far eastern end were tasked with pushing inland to Caen, a hub city where all the roads in the area converged—whoever controlled Caen controlled transportation in Normandy. Strongpoints, beach obstacles, minefields, and inland

An iconic photograph of British soldiers as they made their way ashore at Sword Beach under thick smoke and enemy fire.

Determined British soldiers climbed off their landing craft and onto Gold Beach near the town of Arromanches.

batteries protected all the beaches. The German 716th Infantry Division and the nearby 21st Panzer Division also defended the area, backed by the big guns on the shoreline that swept north from the eastern flank of Sword Beach.

GOLD BEACH

Twenty-five thousand troops from the British 50th Infantry Division were assigned to the 5-mile stretch code-named Gold Beach. From east to west, the towns of La Rivière, Le Hamel, Arromanches, and Longues-sur-Mer sat along the edges of the narrow beach. The Germans used the resort houses of these once-quaint coastal towns as cover, but the buildings were flimsy and fire prone in the face of naval bombardment. The real defenses here were the beach obstacles, the inland batteries, and the Kampfgruppe Meyer, a mobile unit trained to repulse a beach invasion.

Gold Beach had four assault sectors: from west to east, Item, Love, King, and Jig. (There was also How Sector to the far west, a natural port the Allies wanted to preserve as best they could.) Two side-by-side brigades and the Number 47 Royal Marine Commando attachment got into position to invade the assault sectors at H-Hour, 0725, but before they could go in to land, high winds piled up the water, submerging intertidal obstacles before the engineers could get to them. The rough waters forced the infantry, tanks, and engineers to all come ashore pretty much at once. Sniper fire kept the engineers from clearing any paths. Two companies of Hobart's Funnies tried to land, but 20 of their LCTs hit mines. The explosions only inflicted light damage on some, while others were completely lost.

Although the obstacles proved deadly, enemy fire was relatively light. The bombardment had been successful here, destroying the wooden houses where the Germans had been set up. Men and tanks made their way ashore. As the tide came in, narrowing the beach, the first wave moved inland as the second wave arrived. The invasion proceeded in an inordinately orderly fashion, and some men even stopped to brew tea once they cleared the seawall. Sherman tank commander Lieutenant Pat Blamey recalled, "Everything was well ordered. Things were arriving, being unloaded. All those nice little French villas just inland had been set on fire and almost all were destroyed."

Many of the outnumbered Germans and Russians from the Ost battalion surrendered quickly across Gold Beach, but at Le Hamel in the east, enemy soldiers put up a fierce fight from a pillbox that was supported by inland mortar fire. The buildings in Le Hamel were brick instead of wood, so they had withstood the bombardment better. The Germans managed to put all the Allied tanks in the area out of commission, and the Brits had to flank the town instead of taking it head-on. It was a hard battle, but by midafternoon the British controlled Le Hamel.

JUNO BEACH

The 6 miles code-named Juno Beach were divided into two sectors: Mike on the west and Nan to the east. The 7th Brigade of the Canadian 3rd Infantry took on Mike, and the 8th Brigade stormed

Nan. Courseulles-sur-Mer was in the center (though technically part of the Mike sector), and it was the most heavily defended point of the three eastern beaches.

H-Hour was set for 0735, but command delayed the landing plan to give boats time to clear the natural reefs that bordered the shore. Landings didn't start until 0755, by which time the tide had started to wash over the beach obstacles, which meant the engineers couldn't clear paths. The landing craft carefully maneuvered their way through the "Devil's Garden" of mines atop poles planted in the intertidal sands, but 30 percent of them hit obstacles.

In some areas, there was little enemy fire at first. As the Canadians made their way ashore, they hoped the early-morning bombardment had done its job. But once the men started to hit the beach, the Germans opened up a network of brutal crossfire. The Canadians took heavy casualties, especially in the Royal Winnipeg Rifles and the Queen's Own Rifles of Canada companies. In the first hour of fighting, the men had only a 50 percent chance of making it across the beach. Farther east, enemy batteries opened fire on the landing craft, and men were shot down on the ramps before they even got in the water. As the minutes ticked by, enemy fire increased while DD tanks struggled ashore and provided covering fire.

Sergeant Sigie Johnson of the Regina Rifles saw one of his fellow companymen get shot multiple times but still go on to assault a pillbox. "He shot one of the gunners, and the other one, he got his hands around his throat. He strangled the German, then he died himself, and when we found him he still had his hands around the German's throat."

Across Juno, men came off the boats in conditions that ranged from chest-high water and heavy fire to shallow water with light fire. It was bloody work, but the Canadians pushed across the beach. Sherman

Kampfgruppe Meyer

Kampfgruppe Meyer, the strongest German unit in the area, was nowhere to be seen during the most critical hours of the invasion. At 0400, the commanding officer, General Kraiss, sent his mobile, invasion-ready force to Isigny to chase after an airborne landing that wasn't actually there. At 0800 he called the men back, but it took an hour for the order to reach them and another five hours for them to cover the almost 20 miles back to where they'd started.

The Canadians stormed Juno Beach amidst fierce resistance in the morning, but by afternoon they were pouring onto the shore over an improvised boardwalk.

Late in the day, pack-laden troops easily walked ashore at Juno, but in the morning, that beach had seen some of the worst fighting on D-Day outside of Omaha.

The British Royal Navy cleared beach obstacles at Sword to make inland progress easier. Note the tank dozers in the background.

tanks rolled in and dropped ladders over the seawall, and Crab tanks flailed for mines. Troops cleared the wall and made progress inland to the towns, clearing their first objectives. They linked up with Gold Beach to the west, but Sword Beach to the east was cut off by German opposition. Still more men poured in, and by 1200 all 21,400 troops were ashore. The Canadians had won the day, but at a casualty rate of one in 18, which nearly rivaled that of Omaha.

SWORD BEACH

Sword was a 5-mile stretch assigned to 29,000 troops from the British 3rd Infantry Division. The Germans had put up the usual beach obstacles, fortifications on the dunes, antitank ditches, and mines, but the major defenses for Sword were the inland 88-millimeter gun, the 75-millimeter guns positioned 5 miles east at Merville, and the 155-millimeter guns 25 miles east at Le Havre. Fortunately, paratroopers had captured the Merville guns early that morning.

At H-Hour, 0725, Allied aircraft dropped a smoke screen that blinded the enemy artillery. Infantry and tanks landed first, and engineers quickly followed in their Hobart's Funnies to clear the beach obstacles. The Crabs did their work, going up and down the beach to the dunes, flailing their chains and clearing mines. Major Kenneth Ferguson of the 3rd Infantry Division said, "We were saved by our flail tanks. No question about it."

British regiments swept the four sectors of beach—Oboe, Peter, Queen, and Roger—under moderate fire. By 0800 the Brits were already fighting their way inland. By 1000, they had secured the town of Hermanville-sur-Mer behind the center of the beach. To the east, French and British commandos from the 1st Special Service Brigade pushed through heavy resistance in the town of Ouistreham on their way to link up with paratroopers at the Orne river and Caen Canal at 1300. But to the west, troops faced off with German defenses at Lion-sur-Mer, where they were unable to dislodge the enemy from the battery. Fire continued to strafe the beach, and the Allies needed to clear that area to hook up with Juno Beach. As evening approached, traffic piled up on the sand, and the situation only got worse. By the end of the day, the Brits controlled the beach, but they had a long way to go to achieve their D-Day objectives. Even still, Sword Beach was considered a success with approximately 680 casualties. ■

OFF THE BEACHES

D-Day in the Rest of the World

Transocean, the Nazi news agency, was the first to break the story that the Allies were invading Europe. The Associated Press then picked it up, and it went out on the wire. At 0800, or 2:00 a.m. EDT, radio broadcasts in the United States were interrupted with the message "German radio says the invasion has begun" but warned that there was no Allied confirmation yet. An hour and a half later, at 0932, the Supreme Headquarters of the Allied Expeditionary Forces in London gave that confirmation in a brief communiqué. Then a recording of an eloquent speech Eisenhower had already broadcast to Western Europe went out to New York. He assured occupied Europe, "Although the initial assault may not have been made in your own country, the hour of your liberation is approaching."

The world held its breath as news trickled in. The long-anticipated day had come, and families worried about their enlisted husbands, sons, and brothers, not knowing whether they were part of the secret invasion. The SHAEF would not give out any information on which divisions and ships were engaged in the fighting, so all people could do was wait and wonder. Despite the slow trickle of reports, news chatter was near constant. No one could talk about anything else, even if there wasn't anything new to say.

Houses of worship filled up for special services, and cities stopped for moments of prayer. Eager donors crowded blood donation centers. The stock market took a turn south over fears of losing the booming "war economy." The British and American governments went about their normal business, though President Roosevelt held a press conference in the afternoon stating that "the American naval losses were two destroyers and one LST. And the losses incident to the air landing were relatively light—about 1 percent." An encouraging account, but inaccurate. Prime Minister Churchill talked about the invasion in Parliament, saying, "So far the commanders who are engaged report that everything is proceeding according to plan. And what a plan!"

Special services were held at churches and temples across the world. This New York synagogue offered round-the-clock special D-Day services.

BEHIND GERMAN LINES

Chaos, confusion, and indecision ran rampant behind the Atlantic Wall as Hitler slept until noon.

As news of the invasion spread around the world, Hitler slept. Allied troops had landed on the beaches of Normandy by the thousands, moved inland, and cleared the Atlantic Wall's defenses hours before he would wake. Only his orders could release the dreaded Panzer divisions that had wreaked havoc on the Allies throughout the war, and he wouldn't rouse until noon on June 6, 1944. As fate would have it for D-Day, General Rommel had traveled back to Germany to celebrate his wife's birthday and German commanders from the Normandy beach areas were away from their posts to play war games. This meant that much of the top brass was nowhere near the invasion to assess the situation and give orders, and as a result, the infantry divisions remained largely immobile. Reports of the invasion and orders on what to do about it would have to travel back and forth over great distances as well as up and down a complicated chain of command before troops could take any real action. The slow response time of the Reich

Column after column of soldiers listened to Hitler speak at the 1936 Nuremberg Rally, which focused on Germany's demand to reclaim territories it lost after World War I.

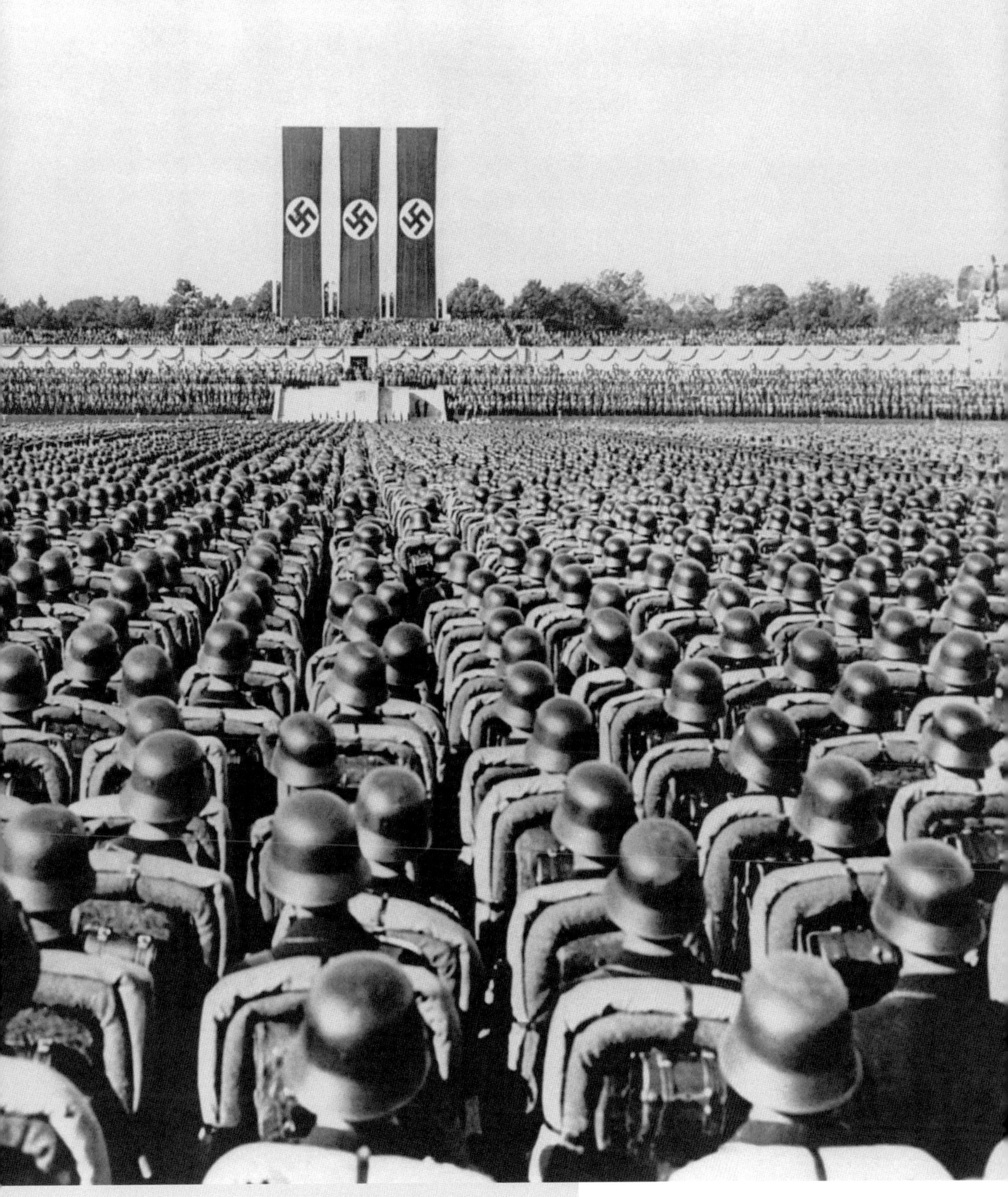

Field Marshal Rommel personally inspected beach obstacles of the Atlantic Wall. His first inspection took place in December 1943, which left him unimpressed with the state of the wall and determined to improve it.

ended up giving the Allies a critical advantage.

IT MUST BE PAS-DE-CALAIS

Operation Fortitude was incredibly successful in convincing the Germans of what they thought they already knew: the Allied invasion would happen at Pas-de-Calais, the port at the narrowest point of the Channel between France and England. Hitler and Rommel poured an immense amount of their resources for the Atlantic Wall here. Millions of mines, thousands of tons of concrete fortifications, and numerous Panzer divisions made Pas-de-Calais an impenetrable stronghold in Hitler's Festung Europa—which is exactly why the Allies would not touch it. Hitler even tried to bait the Allies into invading there by building launch sites for his long-range *Vergeltungswaffen* (Vengeance Weapons), V-1 and V-2 rockets, but he made the trap too dangerous.

As the German High Command watched the putative weapons and troops build up in southern England, they felt reassured that Calais was the target because it was even closer to the English ports than the actual invasion sites. The Calais deception was so successful, in fact, that even after the invasion began, Hitler and other commanders remained convinced Normandy was just a ruse to distract the Wehrmacht from a "real" invasion, and so they only sent in reinforcements slowly and begrudgingly.

ENEMIES IN THE FRONT LINE

The Germans had great confidence in their static Atlantic Wall defenses. The obstacles, batteries, and concrete fortifications were so plentiful and formidable that they didn't require much manpower. Many of the soldiers manning the guns of the Atlantic Wall were in Ost formations, made up of troops that had been taken prisoner from Russia, Poland, and even farther-flung countries such as Korea. The only thing that kept them at their posts was a German officer's gun at their backs.

While there were some highly trained divisions in Normandy, such as the 352nd and a few Panzer formations, many consisted of men who were far younger or older than the ideal age for a soldier. For instance, the average age in the 709th Division was 36.

SCATTERED PANZERS

The Wehrmacht had about 10 Panzer divisions stationed in France, and members of the German High Command disagreed about where to position them. Rommel wanted them near the water because he believed the best place to repel an invasion was on the beach; if the Allies got in, it wasn't likely that the Reich could push them back out. Gerd von Rundstedt, the Wehrmacht commander in chief in Western Europe, wanted them in a central position where they could be mobilized to meet a threat from any direction as it advanced inland. Hitler didn't like giving any one of his military commanders too much power, so he split up the Panzer divisions, giving three to Rommel, three to Rundstedt, and four to a reserve group under General Leo Geyr von Schweppenburg. Only Hitler himself could release the Panzers into action, and on D-Day none were close enough to the invasion beaches to get there quickly.

AS THE ALLIES CAME ASHORE

After enduring a dawn bombardment of thunder and hellfire, three divisions of the 7th German Army, two of which were static, watched the Allies come ashore. The soldiers in the fortifications felt pretty much invincible as D-Day dawned. They were protected by thick concrete walls reinforced by steel. They were unscathed by the Allied bombardment, though they still had to shake off the shock from the bombs before they could man their guns. They had diagrams that showed them exactly where to aim to hit any target within their range, and they inflicted a breathtaking number of casualties on the Allied invaders at Omaha. But "to see tanks coming out of the water shook them rigid," remembered Canadian Sergeant Leo Gariepy, who drove a DD tank onto Juno Beach.

As the invasion progressed, confusion spread down the German line. Some soldiers were indeed panicking at the sight of the enemy with its swimming tanks. Others held fast to their guns. Many Ost troops looked for ways to surrender. The mobile infantry had been running around since the wee hours of the day, trying to fend off the paratrooper

This view down Omaha Beach was captured from inside a German gun emplacement. It shows how the 88-millimeter guns were positioned to fire across the beach at landing troops.

This Tiger tank from the 1st Panzer Division rolled across France in April 1944. The Panzer divisions in France were split up under three different commanders, but Hitler was the only one who could release them into action.

"TO SEE TANKS COMING OUT OF THE WATER SHOOK THEM RIGID." —SERGEANT LEO GARIEPY

Hitler had made a rat's nest out of his chain of command, and the slow, confused orders that came down on D-Day allowed the Allies to get the foothold they needed.

Flag bearers marched in unison at the Reichsparteitag, the Nuremberg Rally held annually to promote the ideals of the Nazi Party.

landings, which were themselves so chaotic that they threw the German defenses into even further disarray. Reports of Allied invading forces came in from all over, many of them inaccurate. Some groups, like Kampfgruppe Meyer from Gold Beach, hiked for miles only to find themselves at a destination devoid of enemy troops. Then they had to hike back to the real action. To add to the chaos, many of the German division commanders didn't get to their posts until late in the day because, ironically, they had been on their way to a war game that was supposed to simulate an Allied invasion.

SLOW TO ACT

The confusion extended up the chain of command as Hitler slept and Rommel remained out of communication. The chain of command itself was a puzzle of Hitler's own making; because he distrusted his own generals, he kept all the power of command that he could to himself. This would be one part of his undoing.

Very early on D-Day, Rundstedt realized the invasion was a real crisis. He ordered two Panzer divisions to head toward Normandy hours before the first Allied boot had even hit the beach. But he didn't command the Panzers; Hitler did. So they sat. And they waited.

When Hitler finally did get up and was informed of the invasion, he said, "The news couldn't be better. As long as they were in Britain, we couldn't get at them. Now we have them where we can destroy them." And maybe he would have if he had acted faster. But Hitler didn't give the order for the Panzers to move out until 1600, and even then he wasn't convinced he was facing the real invasion. For days, he thought Normandy was a feint and the real invasion would be crossing to Pas-de-Calais at any moment. He held reserves for this "real" invasion even as more and more Allies poured onto the Normandy shores.

In all this confusion, the Germans mounted just one Panzer counterattack late on D-Day, and the Allies repulsed it. In the crucial days to come, the German reinforcements that were sent into Normandy were too weak to push out the Allies, who had come to stay. ■

"AS LONG AS THEY WERE IN BRITAIN, WE COULDN'T GET AT THEM. NOW WE HAVE THEM WHERE WE CAN DESTROY THEM." —ADOLF HITLER

AT THE END OF THE DAY

Across Normandy, exhausted Allied troops dug in for the night. So far, the invasion was a success.

The sun finally set at 2200, a full 16 hours after H-Hour. The Allies had captured all five landing zones. Utah, Gold, and Sword had gone well compared to Omaha and Juno, but each beach had been a hard, bloody battle won through grit, improvisation, and sheer numbers. Roughly 151,000 American, British, Canadian, and Free French troops survived the assault. The breakdown of Allied casualties, however, is hotly debated. Most estimates put the number of casualties—including the dead, injured, and missing—at 10,000, nearly a quarter of those occurring at Omaha. Of the 4,400 men who died that day, 2,500 were American.

The landings had not gone as planned by any stretch, but even that had been expected from the beginning. As Eisenhower himself was fond of saying, plans were everything before the battle but useless once it was joined. At the end of D-Day, the Allies had to assess where they stood. Most units had not achieved the ambitious objectives set out in the original plan, so commanders had to reevaluate where they were and what they should do next.

This Army situation map shows where the Allied and German forces stood at D-Day, 2400 hours. Not all objectives had been met, but the invasion was still a success.

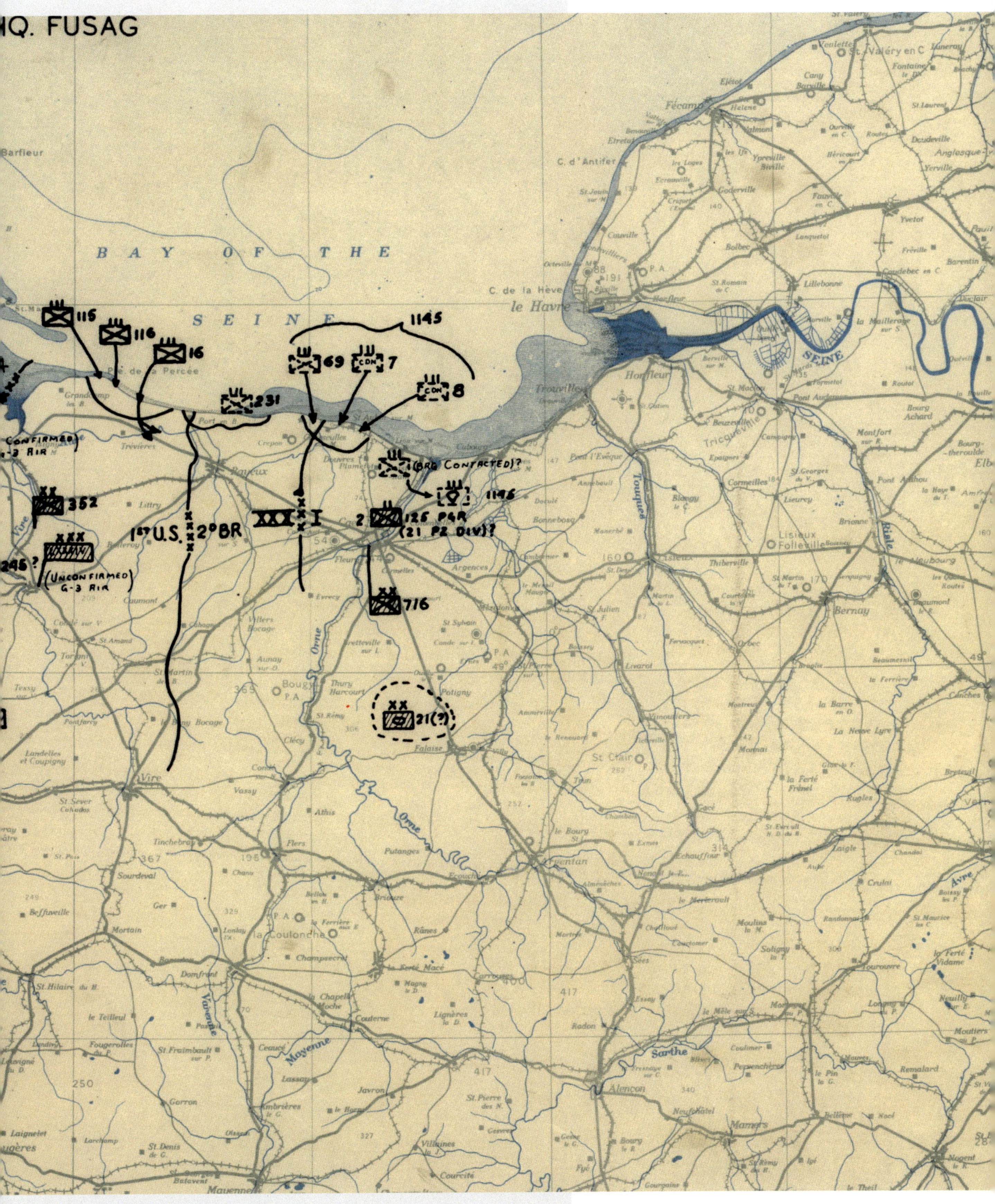
HQ. FUSAG
BAY OF THE SEINE
115
116
16
1145
69
7
8
231
CONFIRMED
G-3 AIR
(BRG CONTACTED)?
1146
352
1ST U.S.
2D BR
XXX I
2
125 PZR
(21 PZ DIV)?
245?
(UNCONFIRMED
G-3 AIR
716
21(?)
le Havre
Fécamp
Honfleur
Trouville
Lisieux
Bernay
Falaise
Vire
Argentan
Alençon
Mayenne
Orne
Seine
Touques
Sarthe
Barfleur
C. de la Hève
C. d'Antifer
Bayeux
Caen
St. Valéry en C
Lillebonne
Yvetot
Bolbec
Pont l'Evêque
Cabourg
Condé sur N
Domfront
Mortain
Flers
Sées
Mamers
Villers Bocage
Aunay sur O
Thury Harcourt
St Lô
Tinchebray
Sourdeval
Lassay
Ambrières
Laigle
Vimoutiers
Orbec
Livarot
Thiberville

This once-deadly German gun was disabled and turned into nothing more than a hook for a soldier's bag.

UTAH BEACH'S UPS AND DOWNS

The 4th Division was one of the most successful forces on D-Day. The landing plan was rendered useless pretty much from the get-go, but the troops took advantage of the mistake and quickly moved across the beach and made their way inland. At H+15, 23,500 troops were ashore with 1,700 vehicles.

The 4th was successful in large part thanks to the work the paratroopers had done in the wee hours of the morning. They had secured much of the area behind the beach as well as the western exits while taking out inland batteries, which greatly reduced the amount of enemy fire the infantry faced. The paratroopers also engaged Germans troops throughout the countryside, which confused the Germans and prevented them from forming a counterattack. (The casualty rate for the paratroopers is unknown because the US Army Air Force did not keep separate numbers for D-Day and those suffered in the weeks to come.)

Infantrymen and paratroopers linked up from noon to nightfall behind Utah. Seabee Orval Wakefield noted, "By middle afternoon, the beach had changed from nothing but obstacles to a small city." While the initial plan had been to secure the coast all the way up to Quinéville, the Allies only controlled up to Foucarville, 5 miles short of their objective. To the south, they accomplished their objectives; they held the lock at La Barquette and a front along the Douve river north of Carentan, including the town of Pouppeville, but their grasp was shaky.

Inland, the Americans held Sainte-Mère-Église, but it had been a tough fight. Germans still held positions north of the town, and when glider reinforcements came in on schedule at 2100, the Germans inflicted heavy casualties on them.

Paratroopers who had landed off target early in the morning were cut off on the western side of the Meredet. On the east bank of the river, troops took and then lost the bridge at La Fière. Germans held on to highway and railway bridges that the Allies had hoped to capture in Carentan, which gave the Nazis mobility for the battles to come.

MOVING INLAND FROM OMAHA BEACH

Command knew from the get-go that Omaha would be the hardest beach to invade. Troops faced a

> "THE BEACH HAD CHANGED FROM NOTHING BUT OBSTACLES TO A SMALL CITY."
>
> —SEABEE ORVAL WAKEFIELD

stretch of shingle that tanks couldn't traverse and then a minefield backed by heavy fortifications. If they made it through all that, they still had to contend with a wall of bluffs that had just a few narrow exits, some of which were little more than dirt paths. Despite seemingly insurmountable hurdles, the 116th and 16th Regiments took the beach, which in itself is an almost miraculous achievement given how the day began.

Their primary objective had been to secure a beachhead from Port-en-Bessin in the west to the Vire river and Isigny in the east, and they did that. From there, the plan grew even more ambitious. Troops were supposed to capture multiple towns as they pushed all the way down to La Tortonne river 5 miles inland. Because

D-Day by the Numbers

UTAH
- 23,500 troops went ashore
- Approximately 300 casualties

OMAHA
- 34,200 troops landed
- Approximately 2,374 casualties

GOLD
- 25,000 troops landed
- Approximately 1,000 casualties

JUNO
- 21,400 troops landed
- Approximately 1,200 casualties

SWORD
- 29,000 troops landed
- Approximately 680 casualties

Omaha Beach was still choked with vehicles, the wounded, and the dead late on D-Day, but the Allies were firmly ashore.

British commandos inspected a destroyed German casemate on the edge of La Rivière.

of the opposition on the beach, many soldiers weren't able to move on these objectives until midafternoon, and once there, the reduced forces faced heavier opposition than anticipated.

They moved in around three towns: Vierville, Colleville, and Saint-Laurent. Rangers and the 116th took control of Vierville in the afternoon, but their hold was weak. When the Rangers tried to press west to link up with their fellow companies at Pointe du Hoc, well-camouflaged enemy fire forced them to call off their operations.

The fighting around Saint-Laurent, behind the center of the beach, began around 1000. German resistance was fierce as troops tried to advance inland across mostly open areas. Small pockets of well-armed, well-protected Germans held elements of five battalions in place for the night.

Near Colleville, the first Allied troops moved inland at 0900. As they approached a German encampment outside the town, they came under heavy fire. The fighting in the area was scattered, and there was little communication between groups. Troops fought from house to house for two hours but were unable to take Colleville as D-Day came to a close. Captain James Robert, aide to V Corps' General Leonard Gerow, said that "around midnight when things seemed to be fairly quiet, I remember thinking, *Man, what a day this has been. If every day is going to be as bad as this, I'll never survive the war.*"

INLAND CHALLENGES FROM GOLD BEACH

At Gold Beach, the British took their first objectives—the coastal towns of Arromanches, La Rivière, and Le Hamel—by midafternoon. But as they pushed inland, their well-organized success did not follow them. They managed to get as far as 5 miles in but weren't able to achieve their secondary objectives—taking Bayeux and cutting off the Caen–Bayeux highway. They were, however, able to link up with Canadians from Juno at the town of Creully and position themselves to take on their objectives the next day. Ronald Seaborne, a seaman from the light cruiser HMS *Belfast*, was separated from his party as they moved inland. He found himself in a small church graveyard in a shootout with a German soldier. "I got a lucky ricochet on my enemy, who slumped from his hiding place into my full view. I went over and looked at him and found I was gazing at a young boy, presumably one of the Hitler *Jugend*. I felt sick."

HARD-FOUGHT JUNO BEACH

The worst of the fighting for the Eastern Task Force happened during the morning at Juno Beach. Even so, by 1200, the full force of 21,400 Canadian troops was ashore and clearing its first objectives in the coastal towns. After a grueling day at sea, hard fighting on the beach, and hiking into towns, many troops decided to dig in short of their final objectives. It was either that or move on to face German units who were better trained than those the Canadians had faced on the beach, including the 21st Panzer Division. Private Gerald Henry of the Royal Winnipeg Rifles recalled, "My first day in France was one of amazement. I seemed to always be far enough away from danger, yet always a part of it."

One troop from the Canadian 1st Hussars Tank Regiment did push almost 10 miles inland and gained the Caen–Bayeux highway. It was the only unit to reach its final D-Day objective, and it was a short-lived triumph. The infantry had not been able to keep up with the tanks, so the Hussars had to pull back for the night.

At 1100, the North Nova Scotia Highlanders had landed with the express objective of capturing the airport at Carpiquet, 5 miles inland. By 2200 they were only halfway there and were ordered to stop for the night.

A COUNTERATTACK AT SWORD BEACH

The British troops at Sword Beach took a lot of prisoners and inflicted heavier casualties on the Germans than they suffered themselves, a rarity in the invasion. By 0800 they were fighting inland, and at 1300 the commandos in the force linked up in the east with the airborne troops

Canadian soldiers lined up German prisoners against a wall in the coastal town of Saint-Aubin-sur-Mer at Juno Beach. Prisoners were often taken on landing craft to be held aboard Allied ships.

"I SEEMED TO ALWAYS BE FAR ENOUGH AWAY FROM DANGER, YET ALWAYS A PART OF IT."

—PRIVATE GERALD HENRY

Troops followed a Sherman tank inland from Sword Beach on the afternoon of D-Day. When the 21st Panzer Division arrived that night, there was tank-to-tank fighting.

British troops were greeted by newly liberated civilians at Lion-sur-Mer in the Sword Beach area.

who had taken the Ham and Jam bridges early in the morning. Major R. Porteous, commander of the No. 4 Commando troop, recalled, "We were still soaking wet, carrying our rucksacks, we really looked like a lot of snails going on."

The British attempted to link up with the Canadians in the west, but that did not go as well as their efforts had in the east. At 1600, the 21st Panzer Division launched the most serious counterattack of the day. The Germans cut into their west flank and moved toward the beach at 2000. There, the Allies repulsed them with airstrikes, antitank artillery, and tanks. Despite their inland progress and battle successes, the British who landed at Sword did not meet their ambitious final objectives to take Caen and the airport at Carpiquet (an objective they shared with the Canadians). ■

MEDALS OF HONOR

Omaha Beach

Jimmie W. Monteith, John J. Pinder, and Carlton Barrett each received the Medal of Honor for gallantry, intrepidity, and going above and beyond the call of duty at Omaha Beach. While their stories are all unique, each of these men undertook great personal risk as they tirelessly performed heroic acts again and again, earning the nation's highest medal for valor in combat for their brave actions on D-Day. (The only other Medal of Honor given out for actions taken on D-Day went to Brigadier General Ted Roosevelt Jr.)

JIMMIE W. MONTEITH,

1st Lieutenant, 16th Infantry, 1st Division

Lieutenant Monteith received the Medal of Honor for going "above and beyond the call of duty on 6 June 1944, near Colleville-sur-Mer, France." His bravery and efforts were truly remarkable. After landing in the first assault wave, he went up and down Omaha Beach reorganizing confused and frightened men "without regard to his own personal safety." He led a group to safety under a cliff, only to return to the beach to lead two tanks through a minefield while he himself remained on foot, unprotected in the open. He then rejoined his company, captured a defensive position on a bluff, and repeatedly crossed 300 yards of open terrain to strengthen his line. The enemy eventually surrounded his unit, and he was killed by enemy fire. His citation notes that "the courage, gallantry, and intrepid leadership displayed by 1st Lt. Monteith is worthy of emulation."

JOHN J. PINDER,

Technician 5th Grade, 16th Infantry, 1st Division

Technician 5th Grade Pinder also earned the Medal of Honor for his actions near Colleville-sur-Mer. He was wounded just yards from his landing craft but continued to carry his "vitally important radio." He struggled through waist-deep water to deliver this equipment to shore. "Refusing to take cover afforded, or to accept medical attention for his wounds, Technician 5th Grade Pinder, though terribly weakened by loss of blood and in fierce pain," went again and again into the rough surf under enemy fire to retrieve crucial communications equipment. He was hit again, but instead of resting or getting help, he remained under open fire to help establish radio communication. He was still working when he was shot yet again, and this time it was fatal. D-Day was his 32nd birthday. His citation notes that "the indomitable courage and personal bravery of Technician 5th Grade Pinder was a magnificent inspiration to the men with whom he served."

CARLTON BARRETT,

Private, 18th Infantry, 1st Division

Private Barrett received the Medal of Honor for his actions near Saint-Laurent-sur-Mer, where he disembarked from his landing craft under enemy fire into water up to his neck. After struggling to shore and "disregarding the personal danger," he went back into the surf time after time to save his fellow soldiers from drowning. Under intense fire, he assisted wounded men, calmed those suffering from shock, carried the injured to an evacuation boat, and took messages up and down the fire-swept beach. His citation notes, "His coolness and his dauntless daring courage while constantly risking his life during a period of many hours had an inestimable effect on his comrades and is in keeping with the highest traditions of the US Army." Of those who received the Medal of Honor for their actions at Omaha, Private Barrett was the only one to survive the war. He stayed in the service and rose to the rank of staff sergeant before retiring in 1963.

THE BATTLE OF NORMANDY

Now that the Allies had their foothold in France, they had to do more than keep it—they had to push the Nazis all the way back to Germany.

D-Day was just the beginning of the fight to liberate France. Operation Overlord, far bigger than the invasion alone, lasted through August, as the Allies cleared the German Army from the northern parts of the country. Allied forces made their way down to the Loire River and east to the Seine through skirmishes, operations, and tank-to-tank fighting that eventually forced the Germans to flee France. Only then could the Allies reorganize to plunge into Germany itself and meet the Soviet forces coming in from the east. Stalin got the second front he'd demanded for so long, and when the east and west Allied forces met in Germany, it spelled defeat for the Nazi Reich.

On June 7, D+1, the Allies did not have the continuous inland bridgehead from Carentan behind Omaha to Caen inland from Sword that they wanted. Instead, they had three sections of beachheads. The British and Canadians controlled the area between Caen and Bayeux, but they did not hold the towns themselves. The Americans held the areas behind Omaha and Utah, but they did not link up yet.

Once the Allies had the beaches, men with their supplies rushed ashore by the millions. By the end of the Battle of Normandy, more than 2 million Allies would be in northern France.

US 310

A depiction of the destruction that resulted from the bombardment of Port-en-Bessin on D+1. This painting is by American naval officer and artist Dwight C. Shepler.

Operation Aubery, the battle to close the gap between Omaha and Gold Beaches, started on D+1. The British No. 47 Commandos conducted early-morning reconnaissance and learned what a tough time the Americans had had at Omaha. They decided to attack Port-en-Bessin, the town between the two beaches, from the rear instead of head-on. At 1400, the Navy bombarded the port. At 1600, the commandos moved in, and on D+2, the Allies captured the town, linking Omaha and Gold Beaches.

Meanwhile, the Canadians at Juno faced an attack by the German 12th SS Panzer Division. The Nazi force inflicted heavy casualties but was unable to get a foothold. The Allies linked Juno and Sword Beaches later in the day.

Tugs towed artificial harbors called Mulberries across the Channel on D-Day itself, and on D+1 work began to install them at Arromanches and Omaha Beach. These engineering marvels allowed troops and matériel to pour into France while the Allies wrestled the port at Cherbourg from the Nazis.

JUNE WEARS ON

A week after D-Day, Eisenhower was touring the beachhead with his son John. Traffic was backed up on the roads, and men walked around in the open. John, who had graduated from West Point on D-Day, commented, "You'd never get away with this if you didn't have air supremacy." Eisenhower replied, "If I didn't have air supremacy, I wouldn't be here." The Eisenhowers made an important point: if the Luftwaffe had had the strength to launch forceful aerial assaults, the Allies wouldn't have been able to progress inland. Even with control of the air and sea in northern France, it took the Allies another week to link Utah and Omaha Beaches. The Germans held tight to Carentan on the Vire river between the two beaches because they needed the town to bring in reinforcements and supplies. They did manage to launch an attack at Carentan, but the 101st Airborne beat it back from June 8 to June 14. After that, the Allies secured the town.

By mid-June, the Allies had linked all five beaches, forming a bridgehead that went as deep as 15 miles inland. Thanks to the damage the Transportation Plan inflicted on the French railway system, the Allies got supplies and reinforcement onto the beaches faster than the Germans could transport them over land. The Allies mounted new operations to keep progressing inland, but the going was tough. And slow.

Northern France was laced with farmland called bocage bordered by hedgerows up to 10 feet thick. The narrow roads between them choked troop movement.

The British tried to take Villers-Bocage on June 13, but the Germans shut them down. British forces suffered another defeat when they tried to capture Caen in Operation Epsom (June 26–30). Despite the Allied loss at Caen, however, the tank-to-tank fighting inflicted heavy losses on the Germans, which gave the Allies an important advantage down the line. They could resupply and reinforce

Instability in the German High Command

As the German garrison in Cherbourg surrendered, Friedrich Dollmann, commander of the German Seventh Army, suddenly died. Officially, the cause of death was heart attack, though it's commonly believed that he in fact died by suicide. On July 17, a British fighter plane opened fire on Erwin Rommel's car, and Rommel was severely wounded. Gerd von Rundstedt, longtime commander of the western front, believed the war was over after the Nazis had lost so many tanks at Caen. Hitler dismissed him for his doubts. Günther von Kluge replaced him but soon saw Rundstedt had been right—they were going to lose. Kluge took part in the July Plot, an assassination attempt Hitler's own officers made on their leader. Hitler took revenge on anyone even suspected of knowing about the plot, which led to Kluge's suicide on August 19 and Rommel's in October.

British troops tried to use the dense hedgerows to their advantage, but the thick shrubbery turned out to be one of the biggest obstacles in the Battle of Normandy.

Troops were able to just walk onto Utah Beach on D+1—a vastly different experience from the previous day.

A wrecked British tank outside Caen. Both the Nazi and Allied forces lost many tanks in the fighting around this city.

at a rate the Germans had no hope of matching.

Operations on the American front, on the other hand, made better progress, in part because the armored German forces were in the east fighting the British. The Americans cut off the Cotentin Peninsula and advanced on Cherbourg, which they liberated on June 27.

SLOW PROGRESS IN JULY

On the eastern flank of the invasion, the city of Caen had been a D-Day objective. At the start of July, it was still under German occupation. The Allies took the northern end of the city in Operation Charnwood on July 9, but the Germans held on to the rest of the city. The British launched Operation Goodwood on the 18th to try again to take the rest of Caen. Their armored divisions circled east and then headed south, where they faced off against German armored divisions on July 20. The British forces gained some territory but were still unable to penetrate the southern end of the city. Major Bill Close, commander of A Squadron, 3rd Royal Tank Regiment, recalled, "Within seconds, fifteen of our tanks were stationary and on fire. All attempts to turn aside to left or right failed. By late afternoon we had only a few tanks left that were still intact." Both sides lost a great many tanks—which, as before, was worse for the Germans than the Allies.

"YOU'D NEVER GET AWAY WITH THIS IF YOU DIDN'T HAVE AIR SUPREMACY." —JOHN EISENHOWER

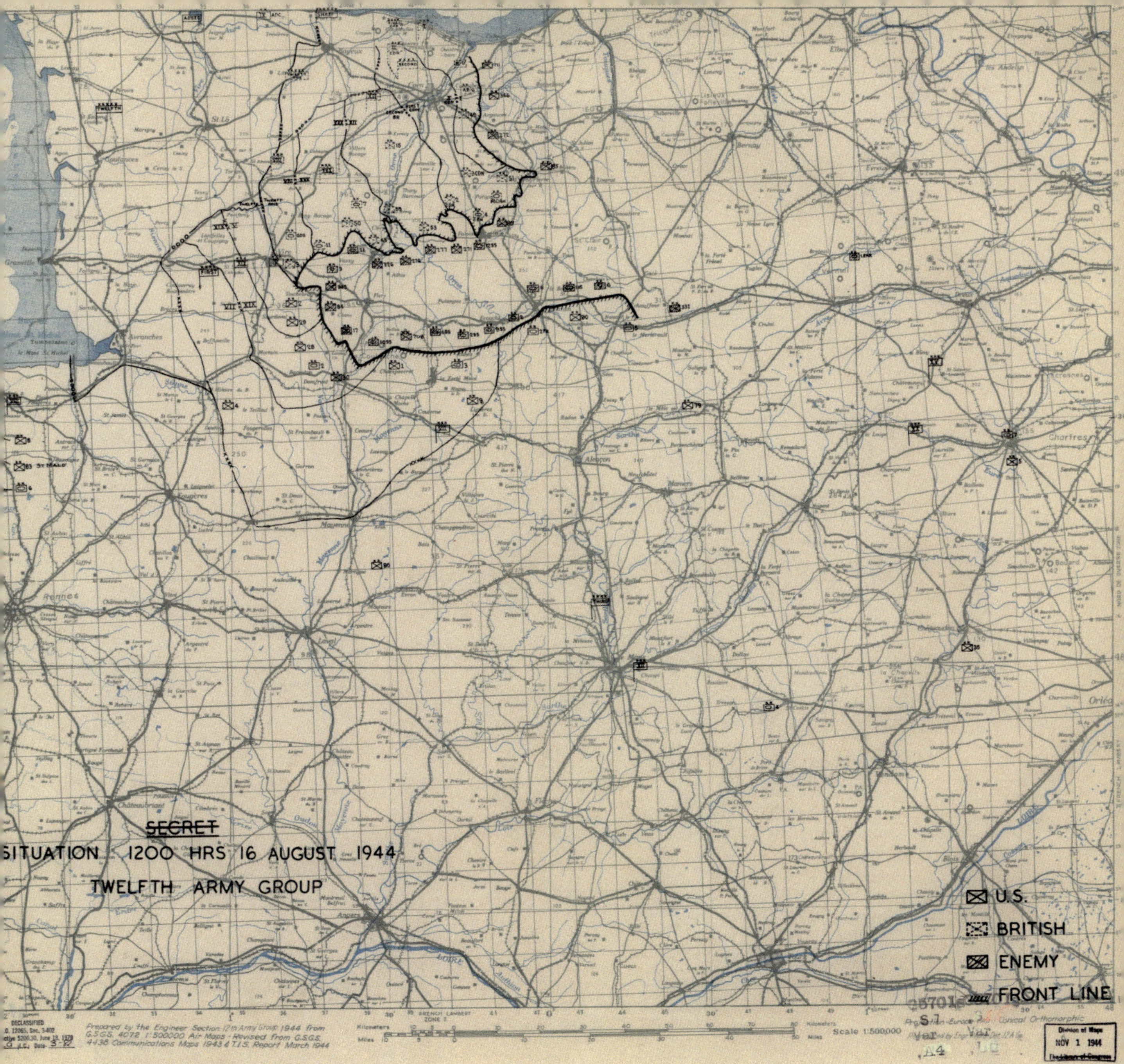

This situation map from August 16 shows the famous Falaise Pocket that caused the German retreat and the ultimate end of the Battle of Normandy.

A few days later, the First United States Army, commanded by General Omar Bradley, launched Operation Cobra in the west. The Americans had already cut off the northern area of the Cotentin Peninsula, but moving south through the hedgerows and pockets of resistance was slow, bloody work, and the Americans suffered heavy casualties. Operation Cobra took advantage of the fact that the German armored divisions were still engaged with the British in the east, and US troops broke through the German forces that had penned them into the peninsula. The Americans then advanced their line south to Avranches, which they liberated on July 30.

AUGUST SEES THE END OF OVERLORD

At the start of August, General George Patton arrived in the Avranches area with his newly recommissioned Third Army. They spearheaded south into Brittany and then circled around the rear of the German forces in Normandy. They marched east toward Caen and the other Allied forces in Normandy marched to meet them. Hitler sent some of his remaining armored divisions west, hoping to cut into the advancing spearhead, but to no avail.

On August 8, the Allied forces were ordered to converge on the

Allied troops marched triumphantly on the Champs-Élysées, Paris, on August 29, four days after the city was liberated and three days after it welcomed home General Charles de Gaulle.

Operation Overlord by the Numbers

The Allies landed more than 2 million men in Normandy over the course of Operation Overlord. Although the exact number of casualties on D-Day is impossible to determine, let alone those during the whole of the Normandy invasion, best estimates put them as follows:

GERMANY

320,000 casualties, with 210,000 missing, 80,000 wounded, and 30,000 dead, though some estimates put the number of wounded as high as 200,000.

UNITED STATES

135,000 casualties, with 106,000 wounded or missing and 29,000 dead.

UNITED KINGDOM

65,000 casualties, with 54,000 wounded or missing and 11,000 dead.

CANADA

18,000 casualties, with 13,000 wounded or missing and 5,000 dead, making a full 27 percent of the invasion's deaths, the highest rate of the Allied forces.

FRENCH CIVILIANS

The civilian casualties in France are incredibly hard to determine and may range anywhere from 12,000 to 20,000.

area of Falaise-Chambois, where they formed the Falaise Pocket and ensnared Hitler's remaining forces in Normandy. The Germans suffered an estimated 60,000 casualties but managed to push through gaps from August 16 to 19; 240,000 Axis troops escaped across the Seine and headed for Belgium as fast as they could go.

As the Germans beat their retreat, the French Resistance rose up against the German garrison in Paris. Eisenhower had initially planned to bypass the city, but as news of the fighting traveled, he decided to send in the Free French 2nd Armored Division to liberate the city. The unit arrived on August 24, and the next day Dietrich von Choltitz, the city commander, surrendered to the Resistance and the commander of the 2nd, Jacques-Philippe Leclerc. Charles de Gaulle, head of the Free French Army, paraded down the Champs-Élysées on the 26th.

The Allies continued to push through France. The Normandy forces of the north met up with their compatriots who had come up from the Riviera in the south. The liberation of France was complete, and the Allies now turned their eyes eastward toward Germany. ■

ENGINEER MARVELS

Mulberry Harbors

One big question faces any beach invasion: how do you get enough men and supplies onto the beaches without control of a port? The Allies' answer? Build their own port. During the planning phase of Operation Overlord, the Allies came up with transportable floating harbors they called Mulberries. They were designed to allow a steady stream of 7,000 tons of matériel to flow into France every day.

Once the invasion began, tugboats towed these engineering masterpieces across the Channel. The navy scuttled 32 merchant ships to act as breakwaters and antiaircraft gun platforms to protect the Mulberries. Engineers installed floating breakwaters and sunken caissons to further guard the harbors. Mulberry A was built off Saint-Laurent, Omaha Beach, and B was constructed off Arromanches (Gold Beach). Combined, they constituted 7 miles of steel roadways that floated on pontoons called Beetles and terminated in pierheads known as Spuds. The caissons alone were made of 600,000 tons of concrete and 31,000 tons of steel—a tall order of materials during wartime.

Ships docked at Mulberry A starting on June 16, three days earlier than planned. Mulberry B was still under construction when a violent storm walloped the coast on June 19. Ships crashed into piers and capsized caissons as the breakwaters came apart at Omaha. Mulberry A was destroyed. The parts that could be salvaged were sent to complete B. By the end of the war, more than 2.5 million men, 500,000 vehicles, and 4 million tons of supplies were transported into Europe via Mulberry B.

While the planners thought the artificial harbors would only be in use for about three months, until a French port was liberated, they were used for 10 months. Remnants of the block ships and caissons remain today. Fifteen percent of the matériel used in Operation Overlord came in over the Mulberries. The rest came in right onto the beaches. Historians and after-action reports have debated whether the Mulberries were worth the immense resources they required. Whether or not the Allies truly needed the artificial harbors to get supplies into France might be beside the point, however. The Mulberries answered the big question of how the Allies could get supplies on shore before they had captured a major port. The harbors may have fallen short of their promise in the end, but in the beginning, they offered a solution the Allies needed before they could start the invasion. Perhaps that was their greatest contribution.

Mulberry A off Omaha shown in full operation. Engineers were able to construct it more quickly than planned, but a storm took it out of commission shortly after it was built.

D-DAY TODAY

June 6, 1944, was a defining moment in American history, and it remains a pillar of our identity.

D-Day is often cited as *the* climactic moment of World War II. While the tide was already turning in favor of the Allies, and Germany's defeat seemed to be just a matter of time, D-Day was a decisive moment that showed the world there really was light at the end of the tunnel. It was a show of force on a scale never seen before, with almost 400,000 men participating in the invasion day. A massive amount of blood was shed on both sides, but morale shifted. The Germans would soon be on the run with the Allies in hot pursuit.

After the war was won and details about D-Day slowly came out, the stories shaped how the rest of the world perceived Americans and how we saw ourselves. American troops showed a sheer force of will, bravery, and sense of duty on D-Day that put them in the ranks of the most heroic men in history. You could drop one of our GIs into a foreign country in the face of a war machine's best defenses, and he would win the day at any cost in the name of freedom. This sense of determination, courage, and self-sacrifice to defend a tenet of our nation's foundation has become an integral part of the American psyche. We became known as a nation capable of anything.

In the 75 years since D-Day, countless books, movies, articles, photos, personal histories, ceremonies, and monuments have memorialized the sacrifice made by the soldiers on the beaches of Normandy. These well-deserved tributes give us a window into the astonishing events of June 6, 1944, one of the most important days in modern history. They also remind us how deeply devoted to freedom we are as a nation and how strong we are when we stand together and with our allies who are willing to pay the ultimate price for that freedom. As President Ronald Reagan said at the 40th anniversary ceremony at the Pointe du Hoc Memorial, "Strengthened by their courage, heartened by their valor, and borne by their memory, let us continue to stand for the ideals for which they lived and died."

"STRENGTHENED BY THEIR COURAGE, HEARTENED BY THEIR VALOR."

—PRESIDENT RONALD REAGAN

The Ranger Monument at Pointe du Hoc was erected by the French to honor Rudder's Rangers. It is a granite pylon that stands on top of the German bunker that many rangers lost their lives taking and defending.

MEREDITH SPECIAL INTEREST MEDIA
Vice President & Group Publisher Scott Mortimer
Vice President, Group Editorial Director Stephen Orr
Vice President, Marketing Jeremy Biloon
Executive Account Director Doug Stark
Director, Brand Marketing Jean Kennedy
Sales Director Christi Crowley
Associate Director, Brand Marketing Bryan Christian
Senior Brand Manager Katherine Barnet

Editorial Director Kostya Kennedy
Creative Director Gary Stewart
Director of Photography Christina Lieberman
Editorial Operations Director Jamie Roth Major
Manager, Editorial Operations Gina Scauzillo

Special thanks Brad Beatson, Melissa Frankenberry, Samantha Lebofsky, Kate Roncinske, Laura Villano

MEREDITH NATIONAL MEDIA GROUP
President Jon Werther
President, Meredith Magazines Doug Olson
President, Consumer Products Tom Witschi
President, Chief Digital Officer Catherine Levene
Chief Revenue Officer Michael Brownstein
Chief Marketing & Data Officer Alysia Borsa
Marketing & Integrated Communications Nancy Weber

SENIOR VICE PRESIDENTS
Consumer Revenue Andy Wilson
Corporate Sales Brian Kightlinger
Direct Media Patti Follo
Research Solutions Britta Cleveland
Strategic Sourcing, Newsstand, Production Chuck Howell
Digital Sales Marla Newman
Product & Technology Justin Law

VICE PRESIDENTS
Finance Chris Susil
Business Planning & Analysis Rob Silverstone
Consumer Marketing Steve Crowe
Shopper Marketing Carol Campbell
Brand Licensing Steve Grune

Vice President, Group Editorial Director Stephen Orr
Director, Editorial Operations & Finance Greg Kayko

MEREDITH CORPORATION
President & Chief Executive Officer Tom Harty
Chief Financial Officer Joseph Ceryanec
Chief Development Officer John Zieser
President, Meredith Local Media Group Patrick McCreery
Senior Vice President, Human Resources Dina Nathanson

Chairman Stephen M. Lacy
Vice Chairman Mell Meredith Frazier

TANDEM BOOKS INC.
www.tandem-books.com
Creative Director Ashley Prine
Editorial Director Katherine Furman
Historical Consultant Steven Weingarter

Published by Meredith Special Interest Media
225 Liberty Street • New York, NY 10281

PICTURE CREDITS
Top (t), Bottom (b)
1, 2 (b), 3, 4, 45 (b), 73, 76, 77, 92, 93 © Everett Historical/Shutterstock
2 (t), 17, 33, 56 (b), 57, 63 (b), 88 courtesy of the National Archives & Records Administration
7, 8, 10, 12, 29, 38 (b), 71, 79, 87, 91 courtesy of the Library of Congress
9 © SARYMSAKOV ANDREY / Shutterstock
11 © Photo 12 / Alamy Stock Photo
13 © Everett – Art / Shutterstock
14 © Kartouchken / Shutterstock
15, 22, 30 (t), 82, 83, 84 (b) © Military History Collection / Alamy Stock Photo
16 © PJF Military Collection / Alamy Stock Photo
18, 19, 70 (t), 74 © Prisma by Dukas Presseagentur GmbH / Alamy Stock Photo
21, 23, 24, 25, 39, 40, 52, 54, 58, 60 (b), 64, 65, 70 (b), 75 (t), 80, 81, courtesy of the US Navy / National Archives & Records Administration
26, 38 (t) courtesy of the US Naval History and Heritage Command
27 © Peter Hermes Furian / Shutterstock
30 (b) © Everett Collection Historical / Alamy Stock Photo
31 © Frank Naylor / Alamy Stock Photo
32, 44–45 courtesy of the Center of Military History, US Army
34, 37, 67, 84 (t), 89 © Pictorial Press Ltd / Alamy Stock Photo
35 © incamerastock / Alamy Stock Photo
41 courtesy of the Dwight D. Eisenhower Library; National Archives and Records Administration
43, 47, 48 (b), 55, 59, 60 (t), 63 (t), 90 (t) courtesy of the US Army Signal Corp / National Archives
46 (b) © Sue Martin / Shutterstock
46 (t) © Dennis van de Water / Shutterstock
48 (t), 69 © Everett Collection Inc / Alamy Stock Photo
49 © History and Art Collection / Alamy Stock Photo
51, 53, 56 (t), 62 courtesy of the US Coast Guard / National Archives & Records Administration
61 courtesy of Rear Admiral Kenneth Loveland, USN. U.S. Naval History and Heritage Command Photograph
68 © Trinity Mirror / Mirrorpix / Alamy Stock Photo
70 (b) © War Archive / Alamy Stock Photo
75 (b) © michael cremin / Alamy Stock Photo
90 (b) © Sueddeutsche Zeitung Photo / Alamy Stock Photo
95 © Michael R Evans / Shutterstock
96 © Luboslav Tiles / Shutterstock

The Normandy American Cemetery at Colleville-sur-Mer is located on a bluff that overlooks Omaha Beach. The bodies of 9,380 American soldiers who died in France during the D-Day invasion and over the course of Operation Overlord are laid to rest there. Among them are Medal of Honor recipients Brigadier General Ted Roosevelt Jr. and 1st Lieutenant Jimmie Monteith.